Language and

G000124099

Language and Meaning provides a clear, accessible and unique per-spective on the philosophical and linguistic question of what it means to mean. Looking at relationships such as those between literal and non-literal meanings, linguistic form and meaning, and language and thought, this volume tackles the issues involved in what we mean and how we convey it. Divided into five easy-to-read chapters, it features:

- Broad coverage of semantic, pragmatic and philosophical approaches, providing the reader with a balanced and compre-hensive overview of the topic;
- Frequent examples to demonstrate how meaning is perceived and manipulated in everyday discourse, including the importance of context, scientific studies of human language, and theories of pragmatics;
- Topics of debate and key points of current theories, including references to ongoing controversies in the field;
- Annotated further reading, allowing students to explore topics in more detail.

Aimed at undergraduate students with little or no prior knowledge of linguistics, this book is essential reading for those studying this topic for the first time.

Betty J. Birner is a professor in the Department of English at North-ern Illinois University, USA.

Routledge Guides to Linguistics

Routledge Guides to Linguistics are a set of concise and accessible guidebooks which provide an overview of the fundamental principles of a subject area in a jargon-free and undaunting format. Designed for students of linguistics who are approaching a particular topic for the first time, or students who are considering studying linguistics and are eager to find out more about it, these books will both introduce the essentials of a subject and provide an ideal springboard for further study.

This series is published in conjunction with the Linguistic Society of America. Founded in 1924 to advance the scientific study of language, the LSA plays a critical role in supporting and disseminating linguistic scholarship both to professional linguists and to the general public.

Series Editor

Betty J. Birner is a Professor of Linguistics and Cognitive Science in the Department of English at Northern Illinois University.

Titles in this series:

Language in Children
Eve V. Clark

Ebonics
Sonja Lanehart

Why Study Linguistics?
Kristin Denham and Anne Lobeck

Language and Meaning
Betty J. Birner

Is English Changing?
Steve Kleinedler

Sign Languages
Diane Lillo-Martin, Sandra Wood and Joseph Hill

Bilingualism
Shahrzad Mahootian

More information about this series can be found at www.routledge.com/series/RGL

Linguistic Society of America

Language and Meaning

Betty J. Birner

Routledge
Taylor & Francis Group

LONDON AND NEW YORK

First published 2018
by Routledge
2 Park Square, Milton Park, Abingdon, Oxon OX14 4RN

and by Routledge
711 Third Avenue, New York, NY 10017

Routledge is an imprint of the Taylor & Francis Group, an informa business

British Library Cataloguing-in-Publication Data
A catalogue record for this book is available from the British Library

Library of Congress Cataloging-in-Publication Data
Names: Birner, Betty J., author.
Title: Language and meaning / Betty Birner.
Description: First edition. | New York : Routledge, 2018. |
   Series: Routledge guides to linguistics | Includes
   bibliographical references and index.
Identifiers: LCCN 2017036304 | ISBN 9781138218239
   (hardcover : alk. paper) | ISBN 9781138218246
   (softcover : alk. paper) | ISBN 9781315148250 (ebook)
Subjects: LCSH: Semantics. | Semantics (Philosophy)
Classification: LCC P325 .B47 2017 | DDC 401/.43—dc23
LC record available at https://lccn.loc.gov/2017036304

ISBN: 978-1-138-21823-9 (hbk)
ISBN: 978-1-138-21824-6 (pbk)
ISBN: 978-1-315-14825-0 (ebk)

Typeset in Times New Roman
by Apex CoVantage, LLC

For the EELS,
with gratitude,
and in memory of Ellen

Contents

Acknowledgements

Any list of acknowledgements is necessarily incomplete; it would be impossible to list all those who inspired me, taught me, stimulated my thoughts, or encouraged my education. I'm profoundly grateful to be in a position to teach others, as I have been taught by others. I continue to believe in education as a means to change the world.

I am especially grateful to Lenny Clapp, Polly Jacobson, and Jeff Kaplan for deep, extensive, and thoughtful comments that have greatly improved the content of this text. Thanks are also due to Barbara Abbott, Ryan Doran, Larry Horn, Jennifer Justice, Shahrzad Mahootian, and Gregory Ward for comments and discussions that have helped to shape this book. I thank the members of my Spring 2017 Semantics class for their feedback. And Nadia Seemungal and the crew at Routledge have been terrific to work with.

I thank my husband, Andrew, for saving my hide on the technological front innumerable times. He and my daughter, Suzanne, bring joy to my life and keep me grounded, and are the most important people in my world. I thank them both for, well, everything.

I thank my cat, Sammy, for occasionally moving off the keyboard so I could type.

My students are the reason this book exists, and you, the reader, are the reason it has meaning. Thank you.

Chapter 1

Introduction

What is meaning? That sounds like a fairly philosophical question, and it is; but it's also a linguistic one. We say that life has meaning, but we also say that words have meaning. Is it the same kind of meaning? This book is about the second type of meaning – the meanings of words and sentences. So it won't help you understand the meaning of life (sorry), but it will help you understand the meaning of the word *life*, and what happens when two or more people attempt to communicate linguistically.

When we talk to another person, we think of our words as conveying meaning – but a little thought might convince you that this isn't what happens at all. In the most literal sense, when I speak to you, nothing leaves my head and enters yours; nothing is really 'conveyed' except for sound waves. So what is this 'meaning' that we feel we're somehow giving to the other person, and how does it get to them? Human relationships are so fundamentally grounded in language and communication that it's worth considering exactly what meaning is and how it works – as well as what sometimes causes it to go wrong.

In this book, we'll consider what it means to mean. In this first chapter, we'll consider the surprisingly large number of things that the word *mean* can mean. We'll look at the difference between linguistic and non-linguistic meaning, and at the difference between the literal meanings of words and sentences and how these can be used to 'mean' a much greater range of things. We'll look more broadly at the field of linguistics, the scientific study of human language, and what it can tell us about how linguistic form and meaning are related. In Chapter 2, we'll look at the philosophy of language: the relationship between language and thought, the location and types of meaning, and the relationship between meaning and truth. In Chapter 3, we'll consider the literal meanings of words and sentences, what it really means to know the meaning of a word, how meanings can be represented, and how simple meanings are built up into more complex meanings. In Chapter 4, we'll dig more deeply into the question of how speakers use these literal meanings to convey their intended meanings, which can sometimes be quite different from what they've literally said. We'll see how theories of pragmatics can help to explain how hearers infer what speakers intended, even if what they've literally said seems quite different. At the same time, we'll see how this process of inference leaves the door open for these inferences to be mistaken, resulting in miscommunication and misunderstanding: Sometimes our hearer just doesn't get our meaning at all. Chapter 5 will summarize the previous chapters and wrap up.

What does it mean to mean?

To dive right into the deep end of the pool, let's start with the meaning of *meaning*. The first thing to notice is that there's obviously a difference between the word *meaning* and what it, well, means – or, to put it another way, what we use it to refer to. (Throughout this book, I'll use italics for linguistic items like words, so that it's clear when we're talking about a word vs. when we're using it – what's known as the 'use' vs. 'mention' distinction.)

The verb *mean* and the related noun *meaning*, as it turns out, have a surprisingly large number of meanings. Consider the sentences in (1):

(1) a What is the meaning of life?
    b I didn't mean to hurt you.
    c Those dark clouds mean rain is coming.
    d *Dissimilar* means 'not alike'.
    e By *home*, I mean my parents' house, not my college dorm.
    f When I kicked you under the table, I meant that you should stop talking about politics.
    g Those sirens mean a tornado has been sighted.
    h I mean to go to England before I die.

In (1a), the speaker is talking about philosophical meaning, which can be very roughly paraphrased as 'purpose'. In (1b), *mean* could be paraphrased as 'intend' – and the extent to which these first two senses of the word *mean* are related is a complicated matter: *Purpose* in some uses can mean *intent* (as in, e.g., my purpose in going to the store), but not everyone asking about life's meaning is asking whether there's an intent behind it. And in (1c), it's quite clear that we've left intent behind: Clouds do not intend to tell us that rain is coming. In (1d), the word *dissimilar* has a fixed meaning that is not dependent on the intent of the person using it; I can't use the word to mean whatever I want. On the other hand, as seen in (1e), I can use *home* to mean my choice of a limited number of places. In (1f), we get even more intentionality and more freedom, and a less fixed meaning: Kicking my companion under the table can mean quite a range of things in various contexts, limited only by my expectation that the person being kicked will get the message. And what about (1g)? The sirens don't intend to convey anything, so in that sense this sort of meaning is like that in (1c); on the other hand, they're a conventional symbol we've all agreed on, so in that sense it's like (1d); but then again, by using this siren on this occasion, somebody intends to indicate the sighting of a tornado, so in that sense it's like (1f). And, finally, in (1h) – a use that appears in some but not all dialects of English – we've abandoned all convention-ality; here the meaning is purely an intent, with no sense of one thing standing for another.

In short, we use the word *meaning* for everything from intention-free indication, as in (1c), to indication-free intention, as in (1h), with quite a range in between – in addition to philosophical uses like (1a) and totally distinct uses to mean things like 'cruel' or 'stingy' (as in *Scrooge was a mean man*, which is ambiguous between those two senses).

Setting aside the philosophical sense of *mean* and its use as an adjective to mean 'cruel' or 'stingy', we can distinguish two broad categories of meaning based on the degree of intention involved, which philos-opher H.P. Grice called 'natural' and 'non-natural' meaning. Natural meaning is the sort of meaning we see in sentences like *Those clouds mean rain* or *Smoke means fire* or *That chill in the air means winter is coming*. The relation is a natural one, which is to say that nobody intended it to be that way; it just is. There is no intention involved.

Non-natural meaning, on the other hand, is at least to some extent intentional. Somebody has decided that one thing will mean, or indi-cate, or stand for, another. For example, a red light means 'stop' – but there's nothing natural about that meaning. It's almost hard to imagine because we're so used to this correlation between 'red' and 'stop', but we could perfectly well have decided as a society that green would mean 'stop' and red would mean 'go'. The meaning is a non-natural one, which in turn means that it's intentional: Someone, or some group, intends for this correlation to exist.

So which category does language fall into? You may find it counter-intuitive, but linguistic meaning is non-natural. There's no automatic, natural relationship between the word *song* and the type of melodic arrangement it stands for, or between the word *dog* and the type of canine entity it stands for. After all, *dog* doesn't mean the same thing in French, Urdu, Chinese, or Swahili, all of which have their own words for dogs. The use of the word *dog* for this creature is simply a convention that English speakers have tacitly agreed to. The relationship between most words and what they stand for is arbitrary – there's no reason the word *chair* couldn't have ended up meaning 'canine creature' – but it's conventional, meaning everybody who speaks English has in some sense agreed to use that word for that meaning.

Within non-natural meaning, then, we have linguistic meaning and non-linguistic meaning (like the fact that a red light means that you must stop your car). This book is concerned with linguistic meaning – which, as we'll see, is also subject to various degrees of intentionality, but it's clear that most linguistic meaning is non-natural in that the words and phrases involved bear no automatic relationship to what they stand for.

The one exception is *onomatopoeic* language, which bears some natural relation to what it represents in that the word 'sounds like' its meaning. Many words for animal sounds (such as *cheep*, *hiss*, or *meow*) are thought to be onomatopoeic, as are words for sounds like *crash* or *bang*. However, even these words differ from language to language; a rooster that says *cock-a-doodle-doo* in English says *kukareku* in Russian. So even here, the relationship between the word and its meaning is partly arbitrary and thus non-natural.

Semantic vs. pragmatic meaning: the role of context

We've talked about linguistic meaning as being non-natural and thus being subject to some degree of intentionality: That is, when we speak, we intend that our hearer will understand us to have intended to convey a particular meaning. This 'intention for our hearer to understand our intention' is a crucial aspect of language. It also, of course, leads us down a philosophical rabbit hole, because for language to work, our hearer has to recognize that we intend for them to understand our intention to convey meaning, and we have to intend for them to recognize it, and they have to recognize that we intend that, etc. And yes, it can make your head spin. But there's also a difference between my intention that they recognize the conventional meaning of what I've said and my intention that they recognize what I meant right now by saying it in this particular context. Confused? Consider these examples:

(2) a *Dissimilar* means 'not alike'. (=(1d))
    b When I said *The pizza is cold*, I meant my slice, not yours.

In (2a), the meaning of *dissimilar* is in some sense fixed; I can't use this word to mean just any old thing. The meanings of words frequently change over the course of time, but I'm not free to use the word *dissimilar* to mean 'therefore' or 'aardvark' or 'television' – or, more accurately, I'm free to use it however I want, but unless I use it for the conventionally accepted meaning, I can't reasonably expect that my hearer will understand what I meant. Most of the time, then, I can't use a word or sentence to mean just any old thing. In some sense, of course, that's not quite true (hence the hedge 'most of the time'); you actually *can* use any utterance to mean anything. For example, you can arrange with your spouse before a party that if you say *The dessert was delicious* it will mean 'I'm having a terrible time and I want to go home'. But in most situations the meaning of your utterance is constrained by its conventionally accepted meaning.

On the other hand, I do have a certain freedom within that conventionally accepted meaning. In (2b), *the pizza* means a certain slice of pizza that is salient in the context of utterance, and this opens up the possibility of misunderstanding. The utterance here suggests that there's been just such a misunderstanding – that the hearer thought the speaker meant all of the pizza present in the context, whereas the speaker in (2b) is clarifying that they meant only their own slice. And of course if the speaker says *The pizza is cold* a week later, they will doubtless be talking about another pizza entirely, whereas the use of *dissimilar* a week from now will still mean 'not alike'. For that matter, the word *pizza* used a week from now will still mean something like 'an Italian pie made of a crust and toppings, typically including tomato sauce and mozzarella cheese'. But the specific pizza intended by the speaker will differ. That is, *pizza* will still mean what *pizza* always means; but what the speaker means by *the pizza* will be different. Thus, there's a difference between **word meaning** (or **sentence meaning**) and **speaker meaning**: The meaning of the word *pizza* is more or less invariant, while the speaker's meaning in using that word can vary from context to context.

Meaning that is more or less independent of context (as in the meaning of the word *pizza*) is called **semantic** meaning. Meaning that depends on the context is called **pragmatic** meaning – but be forewarned that this is a rough definition of this important distinction, and we'll be talking about it in great length later on. For example, another way of framing the difference is to say that semantic meaning is **truth-conditional** and pragmatic meaning is **non-truth-conditional**. In most cases, the two distinctions overlap. Consider (3):

(3) I'm cold.

The conventional, context-independent, semantic meaning of this sentence is (roughly) that the speaker is experiencing a sensation of the ambient temperature being uncomfortably low. This is what it means if uttered today, tomorrow, or next week – here, or in Antarctica, or in Florida – and by me, you, or the President of the U.S. If the speaker is in fact experiencing such a sensation, the sentence is literally true; if they are not, the sentence is literally false. That is to say, the conditions under which it is true – its **truth-conditions** – are the same regardless of context. This meaning is **truth-conditional**. (Of course, the person represented by *I* will vary by speaker; if (3) is uttered by the President of the U.S., that's the person who must be cold in order for (3) to be true.)

On the other hand, the speaker could use this semantic meaning to convey any number of additional meanings, which they will count on the hearer to figure out in context. So the speaker in uttering (3) might mean 'please bring me a blanket' or 'close the window' or 'turn off the air conditioner' or 'turn on the heat' or 'cuddle up closer' or 'I regret eating this ice cream' or 'your brother lied when he said the water in this lake was super-warm' or any of a hundred other things, depending on who's saying it to whom and under what conditions. All of these intended meanings are pragmatic, and they're **non-truth-conditional**, which means that you couldn't get away with saying (4):

(4) When you said *I'm cold* just now, that was a lie; you're not eating ice cream!

Because 'I regret eating this ice cream' isn't part of the truth-conditional meaning of *I'm cold*, the fact that you're not eating ice cream (much less regretting it) doesn't mean you've said something untrue by saying *I'm cold*. Which is to say, you can use the sentence *I'm cold* to mean 'I regret eating this ice cream' in a certain context, but whether or not you regret eating ice cream never affects whether the sentence *I'm cold* is true or not; it doesn't affect the truth-conditions of the sentence *I'm cold*.

Most of the time, meaning that is truth-conditional is also context-independent; that is, there's a core semantic meaning to the sentence *I'm cold* that determines whether it is true or false in any given situation, and that core meaning doesn't change from one situation to another. Additional pragmatic meanings (such as 'I regret eating this ice cream') that are specific to the current context (i.e., context-dependent) are usually also non-truth-conditional: They don't affect whether the sentence itself is true, but simply are part of the pragmatic meaning that the speaker intended by uttering this particular sentence at this particular time. Nonetheless, we'll see later on that the overlap between truth-conditionality and context-independence is not perfect.

Linguistics and the relation between form and meaning

Semantics and pragmatics are two subfields of the academic field of **linguistics**, which is the scientific study of human language. Often, if you tell someone you're a linguist, you'll get one of two responses: Either they'll say that you must know an awful lot of languages, or they'll say something like, "Oh, no; I'd better watch how I talk!" But both of these reactions miss the point of linguistics – one more seriously than the other.

It's true that many linguists do know a lot of languages, simply because linguists tend to be people who love languages, and so they're likely to be people who love to learn new languages. But while a linguist is a person who knows an awful lot **about** language, they're not necessarily a person who knows a lot of different languages; the two are distinct. What a linguist does is to study human language scientifically, the way a botanist studies plants. Linguists ask questions like: What does it mean to know a language? How is linguistic knowledge structured in the human brain? How does a child acquire a native language? What properties are possible in human languages, and what properties are impossible? And most relevantly to the purpose of this book: What's the relationship between language and meaning?

The second reaction – "I'd better watch how I talk" – betrays a more serious misunderstanding of linguistics. Although most people say this jokingly (at least in part), most people have had the experience of being told they've said something 'incorrectly' or 'ungrammatically'. So people fear that a linguist may be a card-carrying member of the Language Police who will think less of them if they violate grammar rules they learned in school, for example by ending a sentence with a preposition, using a double negative, or splitting an infinitive. But nothing could be further from the truth. Since a linguist studies language scientifically, linguists don't take a **prescriptive** approach to language, prescribing how people should talk; instead, they take a **descriptive** approach to language, describing how people actually do talk – just as a botanist describes what a plant actually looks like rather than prescribing what they think it ought to look like.

For this reason, when a linguist uses the word **grammatical**, they're not talking about whether a sentence adheres to the kinds of so-called grammar rules you may have learned in school (which people violate all the time); they're talking about whether it adheres to the rules that govern the way people actually use language – most of which they're unaware of. So the sentences in (5) below aren't ungrammatical; they're simply ungrammatical in the dialect known as **Standard English**. They are, however, grammatical in one or more non-standard dialects of English, each of which has its own set of rules.

(5) a My sister ain't got no ice cream.

  b My brother ain't got no ice cream neither.

  c We heading to the store to get us some ice cream.

Standard English is simply one dialect of English, no better or worse than any other dialect, but it's the dialect generally used in government, education, and business, so it's to a person's advantage to be able to use it.

The sentences in (6), on the other hand, are ungrammatical in all dialects of English:

(6) a *Ice cream none got my sister.

  b *Brother my got neither no ice cream.

  c *To the store going we getting for ice cream.

But even though we'd all agree that these sentences are ungrammatical (that's what the asterisk means), in a funny way you can still see what they mean. That is, if you heard someone utter (6a), you might think they were odd, or a non-native speaker, or playing around, but you wouldn't wonder whether their sister's got ice cream. So there's a clear difference between form and meaning: A sentence's form can be wrong (that is, it can be ungrammatical) while its meaning is still discernible, or its meaning can be all wrong despite its form being flawless, as famed linguist Noam Chomsky made clear with the sentence in (7):

(7) Colorless green ideas sleep furiously.

Here, the meaning is a complete mess (nothing can be both colorless and green, for example), but the form is flawless. So clearly form and meaning in language are to some extent distinct. On the other hand, they do interact: The form of the sentence tells us how the meanings of the words are built up into the meanings of sentences. For example, in (5a) above, it's the form of the sentence that tells us that *my sister* is the subject of *got*, so it's the speaker's sister who doesn't have something, rather than, say, the ice cream not having something. And because *ice cream* is in the direct object position, it's the thing that the speaker's sister has (or, in this case, hasn't) got. The notion that the meanings of larger units (like a sentence) are built up in a predictable way from the meanings of smaller units (like words) is called **compositionality**: That is, the larger meanings are composed of the smaller meanings, according to formal rules.

These formal rules are the grammar of the language, and like semantics and pragmatics, they are part of what linguists study. Because I'll be making reference to different aspects of linguistics throughout this book, I'll take a moment now to briefly describe the primary subfields of linguistics. (By the way, *to briefly describe* is what's known as a split infinitive, and 'don't split infinitives' is one of those prescriptive rules that you may recall from your English classes. Every so often it's fun to violate a prescriptive rule just because you can.)

Phonetics is the study of speech sounds – the whole range of sounds that occur in all of the languages of the world. The sounds that occur in English are only a small subset of the full set of sounds that occur in the world's languages. For example, you might know about the African languages that have 'click' consonants; these sounds don't occur in English. Similarly, you might know about French or German vowels that don't occur in English, such as the vowel in the German word *schön* (meaning 'beautiful'). On the other hand, the 'th' sounds that occur at the beginnings of the English words *think* and *that* (which are slightly different) are relatively rare in the languages of the world, and are often quite difficult for non-native English speakers to master. The study of phonetics covers the way in which sounds are produced (articulatory phonetics), the way they're processed by the hearer (auditory phonetics), and the properties of the sound waves themselves (acoustic phonetics).

Phonology is the study of how these sounds pattern in various languages. This involves, on the one hand, which sounds count as the 'same' in a particular language, and on the other hand, the rules for precisely how these sounds will be pronounced in a particular word or phrase. So, for example, in English, /r/ and /l/ count as different sounds, which is why we can distinguish between words like *rift* and *lift*. In Japanese, however, the closest sound to our /l/ counts as one of the possible pronunciations of /r/; in short, these don't count as two separate sounds, and so you'll never see two Japanese words that are distinguished by one of the words containing /r/ and the other containing /l/ in the same position (such as *ray* and *lay*). The two would count as the same word. But on the flip side, English counts an 'aspirated' /p/ and an 'unaspirated' /p/ as the same sound: To see what I mean, say *I potted a geranium* with your hand in front of your mouth, and notice the puff of air when you make the /p/ in *potted*. Now say *I spotted a geranium*, and note that there's little or no noticeable puff of air when you make the /p/ in *spotted*. And yet English speakers consider both to be the 'same' sound – a /p/ sound – and there's no set of two words in English that are distinguished only based on which /p/ they contain. But in Korean, the two count as different sounds – so /pul/ with no aspiration means 'fire', but /pʰul/ with aspiration (that's what the raised 'h' indicates) means 'grass'. And just as a native Japanese speaker learning English might have trouble with the distinction between /r/ and /l/, a native English speaker learning Korean is likely to have trouble with the distinction between /p/ and /pʰ/. Because in English these count as the same sound, and English has rules that tell us whether or not to aspirate that /p/ in a given context, we'd have a very hard time ignoring those rules and producing, for example, an unaspirated /p/ at the beginning of the Korean word /pul/. (Try it!)

Morphology is the study of word structure and development. You may never have thought about the fact that words have structure, but a word like *irreducibility* is made up of four parts: *ir-*, *reduce*, *-ibil*, and *-ity*. Each part contributes something to the word's meaning: The **root** is *reduce*, and we all know what that means. And to add *-ibil* on the end gives you *reducible* (pay no attention to the minor spelling changes between *-ible* and *-ibil*), which means 'able to be reduced'. Now add the *ir-* at the beginning, meaning 'not', and you get 'unable to be reduced'. Finally, throw on the *-ity*, which changes the whole thing to a noun meaning 'the property of', and you get 'the property of being unable to be reduced'. This is also, incidentally, a really good example of compositionality, which I mentioned before. You might think I cheated in adding those pieces in just the right order: How did I know that *-ibil* should be added before *ir-*, for example? Well, sometimes it's clear: There's no such concept as to *irreduce*, but there is such a thing as being *reducible.* On the other hand, sometimes it's not clear at all: If my husband and I have just arrived at a hotel, and ten minutes later I tell him my suitcase is *unpacked*, that's probably a good thing. But if we haven't left home yet, and we need to leave in ten minutes, and I tell him that my suitcase is still *unpacked*, that's a bad thing. In the first case, *unpacked* is interpreted as *unpack* + *ed*, that is, the past tense of *unpack*: I have finished unpacking. In the second case, *unpacked* is interpreted as *un* + *packed*, meaning 'not packed': I have not yet packed for the trip. *Unpacked*, therefore, is an **ambiguous** word, which means that it has more than one distinct meaning. In short, the structure of a word – how it is put together – matters.

Syntax is the study of sentence structure. Thus, it's similar to morphology, but at a higher level. We see a similar sort of ambiguity here, too: If I say *Mary is an American History teacher*, I might mean that she's an American who teaches History (in which case we're interpreting *American History teacher* as 'American + [History teacher]'), or I might mean that she's a teacher of American History (in which case we're interpreting *American History teacher* as '[American History] + teacher'). Another classic linguistics example of syntactic ambiguity is *John saw the boy with the telescope*: Who's got the telescope, John or the boy? All of the examples of ambiguity we've looked at so far are cases of **structural ambiguity**, because the ambiguity results from there being two different structures available for the word or sentence in question. Like morphology, then, syntax is highly structure-dependent: The meaning of the sentence depends on its structure. This again is due in part to compositionality, since the meaning of the sentence is built up in a predictable way from the meanings of its parts (the words) and how they're put together according to a set of rules (the grammar). Syntax will play a role in our discussion of meaning, because of this interplay between the meanings of smaller units and the rules for building them up into larger units with structurally predictable meanings.

Semantics, of course, is a primary focus of this book, but it's also the one of the main subfields of linguistics – the study of literal (or context-independent, or truth-conditional) meaning. As we've already seen, the semantic meaning of a sentence depends on the semantic meanings of its component words and how those words are built up into phrases, and how those phrases are put together to make sentences. I'll have a great deal to say below about word meaning, relationships among words, sentence meanings, and relationships among sentences. We think we know what a simple word like *sandwich* means, but whole court cases have hinged on the precise meaning of such words, and it turns out that people don't agree on what counts as a *sandwich* at all.

Pragmatics is another primary focus of this book, as well as one of the main subfields of linguistics. As discussed above, it has to do with meaning in context, and how we determine what someone really 'meant' by what they said. And here too we'll find compositionality at work: What we take someone's meaning to be will be determined in part by what the surrounding utterances (and the rest of the context) are like. So our interpretation of a discourse is built up from its pieces (utterances) and how those pieces are put together and relate both to each other and to the surrounding non-linguistic context (things like where and when the discourse is taking place). The simplest example is a sentence like *I saw the dog* vs. *I saw a dog*: the determiner (*the* vs. *a*) affects the interpretation of *dog* – i.e., which dog is being referred to.

Those are the subfields of linguistics that we'll be most interested in, but there are many others. The field of **language acquisition** deals with how children are able to acquire such a complex system so quickly and effortlessly (spoiler: many linguists think some of this knowledge is innate). Researchers in **second language learning** study how people learn additional languages and the best methods for helping them. **Sociolinguistics** addresses the differences in language use among different groups, such as dialect differences between different ethnic groups in America, between men and women, or between different regions of the U.S., and how people's sense of identity is connected to their language use. **Psycholinguistics** uses scientific methods to study how people process and interpret language; it's essentially the study of language as a window into the human mind. **Neurolinguistics** is the related study of how language works in the human brain – where the relevant neural structures are, how they operate, and what happens when they are damaged. There are many other subfields of linguistics as well: There are field linguists who travel to remote regions of the world to learn about the languages spoken there, linguists who study writing systems, linguists who study language change through history, lexicographers who document the words of a language by creating dictionaries, and specialists in signed languages, machine languages, artificial intelligence, animal communication, translation and interpretation, cryptology and code-breaking, teaching English to non-native speakers, and many other areas. And in every one of these areas, meaning is a central concern – because when you come right down to it, the central purpose of human language is to convey meaning.

Conclusion

In this chapter we've seen that the notion of 'meaning' is not a single concept, and that even the idea of linguistic meaning covers a lot of territory. In covering what a speaker 'means' and how a hearer comes to understand and interpret this meaning, we need to talk about issues in philosophy, semantics, and pragmatics. Within philosophy, we'll ask questions like: What's the relationship between language and thought? Where does meaning reside? When I use a phrase like *the apple*, what am I referring to – a real-world object, or something in my mind? What if I'm wrong about the object being an apple; have I failed to refer to anything? How do I structure my beliefs? How are beliefs and ideas shared? What's the relationship between meaning and truth?

That seems like a lot to handle, but it's only the beginning. Heading into semantics, we'll talk about what it means to know the meaning of a word, how word and sentence meanings relate to each other, how we can represent word and sentence meanings formally (and why we'd want to bother), how we build sentence meanings out of word and phrase meanings, and how reporting someone else's beliefs and meanings complicates things.

Finally, we'll move to pragmatics – meaning in context. We'll talk about how speakers use a combination of semantic meaning and discourse context to try to convey their intended meaning, and how hearers use some basic shared principles to figure out what the intended meaning must have been. We'll see how some aspects of an utterance are taken as new and informative while others are taken as either already-known or presupposed, and how those assumptions affect the hearer's interpretation. We'll also see how different word orders for the same semantic content (think of *John threw the ball* vs. *The ball was thrown by John*) affect the way that content is interpreted. We'll see how utterances can change the world in specific circumstances (such as an appropriate official saying *I now pronounce you married*). Finally, we'll look at the surprisingly complicated question of how much of a sentence's meaning really is semantic and how much is pragmatic. Throughout, we'll keep returning to the basic question we started with: What, after all, **is** meaning?

Chapter 2

Philosophical approaches to meaning

I said in Chapter 1 that the question 'what is meaning?' is fairly philosophical, and indeed there has been a long history of interaction between the fields of linguistics and philosophy – and especially between philosophy and the linguistic subfields of semantics and pragmatics, the two subfields most closely associated with the question of linguistic meaning. In fact, some of the most influential names in pragmatics are actually philosophers. Philosophy of language is heavily focused on questions of meaning: the relationship between language and thought, the locus of meaning, and the relationship between meaning and truth. In this chapter we will consider all of these issues and more. Due to the brevity of this volume, I will not present a thorough review of philosophy of language (for example, I won't address the question of an innate universal linguistic faculty, or cover the more general theory of signs known as semiotics); instead, we will focus on what philosophy can tell us specifically about meaning in human language.

Language and thought

You might be surprised to learn that the relationship between language and thought has been a hot topic in linguistics over the years. After all, we normally assume language is a tool for expressing our thoughts – for 'conveying' our thoughts to our hearer. But as I pointed out in Chapter 1, we don't actually convey anything in the sense of passing along something from one person to another. Reddy (1979) wrote a highly influential paper describing a pervasive metaphor in

English that treats communication as a matter of putting our meanings into containers and passing them along a conduit to the recipient, who then extracts the meanings from the containers. Reddy called this the Conduit Metaphor, because it treats language as a conduit and words as containers. He gives dozens of pages of examples of this metaphor in use, but a few examples will suffice here:

(1) a I'm having trouble putting my meaning into words.
     b He doesn't convey his ideas well at all.
     c Her argument went right over my head.
     d I really got a lot out of that poem.
     e She really packs a lot of meaning into her sentences.
     f Let me give you those thoughts a little more slowly.
     g Wait – I didn't get that at all.
     h Did you catch that?

You get the idea. (See? I did it again.) In English, it's extremely difficult to talk about communication without talking about 'putting our thoughts or ideas into words', 'conveying them' to the other person, and the other person 'getting them' (unless an idea 'goes right past them', or 'goes over their head', or they fail to 'get it'). The problem isn't in having such a metaphor, Reddy says, but rather in the fact that we act as though we believe the metaphor: We expect books to contain meaning, and we get angry with our hearer for not 'getting' our meaning. (After all, we handed it right to them!) A more appropriate metaphor, Reddy argues, is one in which language is a blueprint passed between people who live in entirely different worlds containing entirely different materials, who cannot see each other's worlds and have only the blueprints as communication. The different worlds are our mental worlds, and the blueprints are language: Miscommunication and misunderstanding aren't something to get angry about, but rather are the norm, because we can't possibly know the other person's mental world and how, in light of that mental world, that person will interpret the linguistic blueprint we've given them. Similarly, books don't contain meaning; they merely contain ink, which again we're stuck trying to interpret on the basis of what our mental world makes available to us. When two people talk, nothing passes between them but a coded pattern of sound waves, which they have to interpret to the best of their ability, based on each person's mental world and their assumptions about the other person's mental world. But they can never enter that other person's mental world to check whether their assumptions or interpretations are correct. The result is that much of our communication is actually miscommunication – but we never know the difference.

My favorite example of this sort of miscommunication involves a conversation between my husband, Andy, and his brother, Paul, in the mid-1980s. Andy had shipped his old stereo system to Paul, and called him up to make sure he had received it. Paul affirmed that he had received it. As it happened, the 'it' that Andy had sent had included several boxes, one of which contained a turntable. The 'it' that Paul received had not included the turntable. Since this was around the time when LPs were fading and CDs were rising as the music medium of choice, for Paul to receive a system with no turntable was no surprise to him. It was only by happenstance that the loss was discovered many months later. As long as Andy's mental world contained a stereo system with a turntable and Paul's mental world contained one without, and they assumed these worlds matched, there was no reason to go down the list and check. Reddy's argument is that this is the situation we find ourselves in with virtually every communicative interaction we have: I tell you I have a cat named Samson, and you add my cat into your mental world, but even if I try to describe him to you in detail, the cat in your mind and the cat in mine will never be exactly the same. We have miscommunicated, and it's nobody's fault; it's the way language works. Fortunately, most of the time we're close enough. Andy and Paul could have gone the rest of their lives without ever knowing there had been a miscommunication, and really, nobody would have been the worse off for it. Your mental image of Samson doesn't get his coloration quite right, but it never really matters.

In short, Reddy is saying that the options that the English language gives us for talking about communication affect the way we think about communication. At the beginning of this section, I pointed out that it seems obvious that there's a relationship between language and thought – but what seems obvious is that thought affects language: We have thoughts, and we encode them in language. So of course what we're thinking affects what we say about what we're thinking. But it seems much less obvious that there would be an influence in the other direction as well – that is, that our language should influence our thoughts, and more specifically that the particular language we speak should constrain how we see reality. But that influence is implicit in Reddy's argument. This notion – that the tools our language gives us affect our thought patterns, and indeed affect how we see reality – is most strongly associated with Benjamin Lee Whorf. Whorf studied under the influential linguist Edward Sapir in the 1930s, and the hypothesis that your language affects the way you see reality is often called the **Sapir-Whorf Hypothesis**, since it had its beginnings with Sapir, who said in one of his papers:

> Human beings do not live in the objective world alone, nor alone in the world of social activity as ordinarily understood, but are very much at the mercy of the particular language which has become the medium of expression for their society. It is quite an illusion to imagine that one adjusts to reality essentially without the use of language and that language is merely an incidental means of solving specific problems of communication or reflection. The fact of the matter is that the 'real world' is to a large extent unconsciously built up on the language habits of the group. . . . We see and hear and otherwise experience very largely as we do because the language habits of our community predispose certain choices of interpretation.
>
> (Sapir 1929, cited in Whorf 1956:134)

Whorf worked with the Hopi, a Native American tribe, and he noticed that some words that are nouns in English are verbs in the Hopi language, such as *wave*, *spark*, *noise*, *flame*, *meteor*, and *storm*. He believed that this affects the way we view reality – that is, that English speakers are influenced by their language to view a storm as a thing, whereas Hopi speakers are influenced by their language to view a storm as a process or event. In a famous passage from one of his papers, Whorf notes:

> We dissect nature along lines laid down by our native languages. The categories and types that we isolate from the world of phenomena we do not find there because they stare every observer in the face; on the contrary, the world is presented in a kaleidoscopic

flux of impressions which has to be organized by our minds – and this means largely by the linguistic systems in our minds. We cut up nature, organize it into concepts, and ascribe significances as we do, largely because we are parties to an agreement to organize it in this way – an agreement that holds throughout our speech community and is codified in the patterns of our language. The agreement is, of course, an implicit and unstated one, *but its terms are absolutely obligatory*; we cannot talk at all except by subscribing to the organization and classification of data which the agreement decrees.

(Whorf 1956:213, emphasis in the original)

Linguists have been arguing for the past 75 years, give or take, about how strongly Whorf actually held this view. The strong view is termed **linguistic determinism**; in this view, your language is a filter that determines the way you see reality. The weaker view is termed **linguistic relativity**; it has been stated in a variety of ways, but in general it states that language influences thought, or (in another formulation) that different language communities see the world differently (with the direction of the influence left vague). The strong form of the hypothesis has pretty much been soundly refuted: For example, there are languages that don't have distinct terms for green and blue, but that doesn't mean the speakers can't see the difference between green and blue, any more than English speakers are unable to distinguish various shades of red. Similarly, Whorf has often been falsely accused of saying that the Hopi don't have a concept of time (an easily refuted notion); what he actually argued was that their language treats time differently from the way English does, and that their way of thinking about time is correspondingly different from that of an English speaker. In English, we treat time as a series of countable objects – minutes, hours, days, seasons, etc. We count up our minutes and our days; we list them in datebooks; we speak of time as something we can save, lose, have enough (or not enough) of, need, or spend. Time is 'stuff'. In Hopi, according to Whorf, time is more of a 'when' than a 'what': Summers aren't countable things; instead, summer is when it is hot and dry. A Hopi speaker wouldn't agree with Scarlett O'Hara when she says, "Tomorrow is another day"; instead, for that speaker, tomorrow is a return of day. Day comes, goes, and comes again – both in the Hopi language and in the Hopi conception of time, according to Whorf.

One so-called fact that is often cited in support of the relationship between language and thought is the idea that Eskimos have hundreds of different words for snow – but this is wrong in a bunch of ways. For one thing, the number seems to keep growing as the myth gets re-told. For another, the direction of the influence is wrong if you're trying to use this in support of Whorf: The (supposed) relationship in the Eskimo case would be a matter of the perception of reality (hey, look at all the different sorts of snow!) affecting the language, not the other way around. But, more importantly, the claimed difference between Eskimo and English just doesn't hold. First of all, there's no single 'Eskimo' language. There are two main groups of Eskimo languages, Yupik and Inuit, and the languages in these two groups allow a great deal of prefixing and suffixing. If you count all the resulting combinations as separate words, well, yes, then you get a lot. But that's like counting English *snow*, *snowed*, *snows*, and *snowing* as separate words. And English also has other words for snow like *drift*, *sleet*, *slush*, *powder*, etc. Linguists have been trying for years to put to rest what one linguist has called 'the Great Eskimo Vocabulary Hoax' (Pullum 1991). It may be that Eskimo languages have more words for different types of snow than English does, but the number has been vastly inflated, and even if there is a difference in number, those who use this as support for the Sapir-Whorf Hypothesis have the influence going in the wrong direction.

To come back around to where this section began, however, you can see how linguistic relativity meshes with the Conduit Metaphor: Reddy is arguing that English treats ideas as objects (which can therefore be conveyed from one person to another), which in turn influences the way English speakers view communication. This follows in the tradition of Whorf, who similarly claimed that English treats time as a set of objects (which can therefore be counted, saved, and spent), which in turn influences the way English speakers view the passage of time. The controversy over the Sapir-Whorf Hypothesis rages on, with plenty of authors arguing on both sides of the issue. As noted above, lacking distinct color terms for green and blue won't make you think the colors of the grass and the sky look identical. On the other hand, perhaps the fact that English offers you the word *pink* will prevent you from thinking of a pink tulip as being a light shade of red, while the absence of distinct terms for light and dark blue will cause you to think of them as shades of the same color (whereas a speaker of Russian, which has distinct words for light blue and dark blue, is likely to think of them as distinct colors). The jury is still out on the Sapir-Whorf Hypothesis, and the truth of it may depend entirely on how strong a view you're arguing for (or against): linguistic relativity, linguistic determinism, or something in between.

Where meaning resides

The Sapir-Whorf Hypothesis is one aspect of the question of how our belief-worlds relate to language. Another aspect is the question of what it is we refer to when we utter a definite noun phrase like, say, *the tall woman*. There are two interconnected questions to be dealt with: First, when we utter such a 'referring expression', what is really being referred to – a thing in the world or something in our belief-world (an idea or a concept)? Second, relatedly, what determines what's being referred to – the semantic meaning of the expression itself or our intentions? At first blush, it might seem obvious that we refer to things in the world, and that it's the semantic meaning of what we say that determines what we refer to (since, after all, I can't generally use the phrase *my refrigerator* to refer to my cat), but it turns out that things aren't as straightforward as they might initially seem.

So let's take again our phrase *the tall woman*. The common-sense view is that someone using this phrase is referring to a particular tall woman in the real world. But let's complicate matters a bit. Consider (2):

(2) The tall woman holding a glass of water is my mother.

Now suppose the speaker is mistaken, and the person being pointed out in (2) is actually holding a glass of vodka, not water. Has the speaker succeeded in referring to this person? After all, *the tall woman holding a glass of water* doesn't describe the person being pointed out, so the speaker can't be referring to an actual tall woman holding a glass of water. Has the speaker succeeded in referring to the person they intended to refer to? Indeed, has the speaker referred to anyone at all?

You might object that this is a minor point, that there's still a tall woman holding a glass, so it's clear whom the speaker is referring to (which is to say, perhaps you're already wavering on the question of whether it's semantic meaning or speaker intent that determines reference). But let's take things a step further. First, we'll look at a variant of a well-known example from Strawson (1952):

(3) A: Did you hear? A man jumped off the Golden Gate Bridge yesterday.
     B: He didn't jump; he was pushed.

Now, what's the referent of *a man* in A's utterance? It seems like it should be the man who jumped off the Golden Gate Bridge, but there is no such man. What about the referent of *he* in B's utterance? The problem is no easier here. *He* would seem to refer back to the man who jumped off the Golden Gate Bridge, but again, there is no such man. In the case of A, you could argue that the speaker at least **believes** there is such a person, but B doesn't even have that belief. A intends to refer to a man who jumped off the Golden Gate Bridge but is mistaken about this man's attributes; B doesn't even intend to refer to a man with those attributes, but rather intends to refer to the same person A has referred to by means of the wrong attributes. Now, let's consider what happens when the speaker is mistaken about even more:

(4) A: Did you hear? A man jumped off the Golden Gate Bridge yesterday.
     B: Yeah, I heard about that. But the person wasn't a man; she was a woman. And it was the Bay Bridge, not the Golden Gate Bridge. And it was this morning, not yesterday. And she didn't jump; she was pushed.

Now, let's assume B is correct. Is the referent of *she* in B's utterance a man who jumped off the Golden Gate Bridge yesterday? Surely not. It seems instead to be the woman who was pushed off the Bay Bridge this morning. And yet it appears that A and B are referring to the same entity – that the referent of *she* in B's utterance is the same person A intended to refer to. In fact, B affirms this by saying *I heard about that.* What's the 'that' which B has heard about? If it's the event that A has recounted, and B's referent is a woman who was pushed off the Bay Bridge this morning, is it safe to say that A's referent is also a woman who was pushed off the Bay Bridge this morning? Can this be A's referent if A is wrong about virtually every aspect of this referent except for the abstract frame of a person recently having dropped from a Bay Area bridge?

Now consider the possibility that there's nothing in the real world that could possibly count as the intended referent, as in (5):

(5)   A: What was that?
      B: What was what?
      A: I thought I heard a noise. Maybe not. Anyway, it's gone now.

Is the referent of *it* in A's second utterance the noise that A may or may not have heard, which may or may not have existed? It's almost the opposite of the tree-falling-in-the-forest problem: If a sound isn't made, can it be referred to?

Now, you may feel inclined to argue that the referent of *it* in (5) is the sound in A's mind or belief-world. This is the approach some linguists and philosophers of language have taken toward meaning, saying that the referent is essentially a construct in the mind of the speaker. Each speaker is said to have a **discourse model** – that is, a mental model of the discourse as it evolves, including all the entities that have been referred to and their attributes. Thus, when one person speaks of a man who jumped off a bridge, and another responds that it was a woman, not a man, and that she was pushed, that referent's attributes in the first speaker's discourse model are updated.

Linguists often speak as though interlocutors share a discourse model, but that's an idealization. As a discourse like (4) shows, it's possible for the interlocutors' discourse models to be quite different, and as we saw in the previous section in the discussion about the stereo system, sometimes the interlocutors never even know there was a difference. (Reddy would say there are virtually always such differences, however minor.)

Heading back to the bridge, suppose **both** interlocutors are wrong. Suppose they conduct an entire conversation about the man who jumped off the bridge, never realizing that in fact he didn't jump but rather was pushed. Suppose, for that matter, that nobody in the world ever learns the truth, and the criminal who pushed the man off the bridge takes the secret to his deathbed. Now everyone who refers to this person as *the man who jumped off the bridge*, from the media to people in casual conversation, will be wrong about this attribute. If we say that reference is fixed by the semantics of the utterance, and that referents are things in the real world, then we're stuck saying that all these people have failed to refer to anything at all. And yet they manage to have perfectly successful conversations, and it's hard to argue that they aren't talking about **something**, and in fact the **same** thing. But then what is that something?

Can we refer to something that doesn't exist? I can talk about the tooth fairy and Santa Claus. I can discuss a fictional character like Harry Potter, and you can easily evaluate the truth of a statement like *Harry Potter is a wizard*. An atheist can hold a conversation about God. There's no contradiction, in fact, in the atheist stating *God does not exist*. And yet non-existence is an odd thing to predicate of something if the referent of your utterance is by definition a thing in the world.

In light of all this, the obvious move is to say that the referent isn't anything in the real world; successful reference clearly doesn't require that there be anything in the real world corresponding to either the semantics of your utterance or your intended reference. So we can safely conclude that the referent is actually a concept in a person's mental model of the discourse, right?

Unfortunately, it's not nearly that easy. The problem is that when I say *My cat is gray and white*, I don't mean to attribute the property of being gray and white to something in my mind; I mean to attribute it to an actual cat in the real world. When a speaker says *A man jumped off the Golden Gate Bridge yesterday*, they mean to refer to someone in the real world, not something in their head. Nothing in the speaker's head has jumped off the Golden Gate Bridge. And when they say *Harry Potter is a wizard*, they intend to refer not to a real-world entity, nor to an entity in their head, but rather to a fictional entity in a discourse model they believe they share with their hearer. And evaluating the truth of these utterances gets interestingly tricky: The truth of the statement *A man jumped off the Golden Gate Bridge yesterday* would seem to depend entirely on whether such a man exists in the real world, but the truth of the statement *Harry Potter is a wizard* depends on whether such a wizard exists in a particular fictional world.

The temptation at this point, of course, is to say that the truth of the statement *Harry Potter is a wizard* depends on the real world too – to the extent that the Harry Potter books exist in the real world and have a description of Potter the fictional character. But notice that in doing so, you retreat back to a position of considering referents to be real-world entities, and you're stuck with the problem of how you can have a referent whose properties you're wrong about, or how you can refer to something that doesn't exist. What if you and your hearer are in the woods, hear a twig snap, and mistake a trick of the light for a bear? You can successfully hold a conversation about *the bear* without ever realizing that there's no bear at all. When you later tell your family *We managed to outrun a bear*, does the phrase *a bear* refer to an actual bear, or to a bear in your discourse model, or to a trick of the light? Surely your intent is to refer to an actual bear, not something in your head or a trick of the light – but no bear exists to be referred to.

This problem is the source of debate between the **cognitivist** camp, for whom referents are cognitive constructs, and the **referentialist** camp, for whom they are real-world objects. (Both of these go by a variety of other terms, but these will do.) And the question at hand is really the broader question of the **meaning** of an expression. That is, there are two intertwined questions here: First, is the meaning of a referring expression its intended real-world referent, or is it what the expression semantically describes (the **descriptivist** view)? Second, if the meaning of a referring expression is whatever the expression describes, is that the same as saying that the referent of an expression is simply a description in the discourse model? To make this a bit clearer, suppose I utter (6):

(6) Garbanzo beans are chickpeas.

Under a referentialist view, the meaning of *garbanzo beans* is the real-world referent of this phrase (that is, the actual garbanzo beans), and similarly for *chickpeas.* But chickpeas and garbanzo beans are exactly the same thing under two different names. So under a referentialist view, (6) means exactly the same thing as (7):

(7) Chickpeas are chickpeas.

This is a problem, because (7) is a tautological and generally point-less thing to say, whereas (6) isn't. (Note, however, that tautologies like (7) aren't always pointless: If Allen states *I thought I'd like this chickpea dish, but its texture bothers me*, Bertie can respond *Well, chickpeas are chickpeas* – meaning, in essence, 'don't be surprised when a particular set of chickpeas has a property that all chickpeas have'.) Some philosophers of language have used such conundrums to declare victory for descriptivism; the speaker of (6) has different discourse-model referents for *garbanzo beans* and *chickpeas*, with different attributes, even if the difference in attributes is something as slight as 'what my hearer thinks of as garbanzo beans' and 'what my hearer thinks of as chickpeas'. In this sense, the expression *garbanzo beans* means something different from the meaning of the expression *chickpeas.* And the whole purpose of (6) would be to say to the hearer, essentially, 'you should combine these two different referents in your discourse model into one'.

But once again, we're not out of the woods, because when the speaker utters (6), they presumably don't take the expressions *garbanzo beans* and *chickpeas* to have different referents in their own dis-course model. And as philosopher Hilary Putnam (1975) has pointed out, it's entirely possible for a speaker to attribute identical properties to what they would consider distinct things. Putnam's example is that he has no idea how an elm tree differs from a beech tree: Both are deciduous trees of North America. Yet if he says something about elm trees (let's say, *Elm trees typically grow to be more than 20 feet tall*), the truth of that statement will depend on whether it's true of elm trees, not beech trees. Thus, he argues, the reference of the phrase *elm trees* when he uses it can't be determined entirely by the description in his head, since that description doesn't distinguish between elms and beeches. Yet the typical height of a beech tree is irrelevant with respect to his utterance. For this reason, Putnam argues that meaning cannot be entirely in the speaker's head.

We will leave this question unresolved, in part because there is still no agreed-upon answer, but also in part because much of the rest of this book will bear on the question of the location of meaning. And we'll return more specifically in Chapter 4 to the issue of reference and how speakers refer. But having raised the thorny issue of ref-erence, it will be useful to make an important distinction between reference and another sort of meaning.

Sense and reference

Let's return to our friends the garbanzo bean and the chickpea. Suppose George has hated all kinds of beans all his life – kidney beans, navy beans, lima beans, you name it. He's never encountered garbanzo beans, but he's heard of them; and because they're beans, he can confidently utter (8):

(8) I hate garbanzo beans.

One day George's friend Nick invites him over and serves him a delicious chickpea salad. George now utters (9):

(9) Wow – I've never had chickpeas before, but they're delicious!

George has no idea that chickpeas and garbanzo beans are the same thing. So George now believes both of the following propositions:

(10) I hate garbanzo beans.
(11) Chickpeas are delicious.

The question now is whether (12) is true:

(12) George believes garbanzo beans are delicious.

On the one hand, George has had garbanzo beans and did indeed consider them delicious. On the other hand, George himself would strongly claim that (12) is false; indeed, *Garbanzo beans are delicious* is not a statement that seems to accurately describe his beliefs. And certainly we'd like to give George credit for knowing what he does and doesn't believe. This problem feels a bit like the above problem of a cognitivist vs. a referentialist view of meaning, yet the problem here isn't quite the problem of whether we're talking about real-world beans or belief-world beans.

Instead, a philosopher named Gottlob Frege proposed the distinction between **sense** and **reference** to handle such problems. Frege used the example of *the morning star* and *the evening star*. Both phrases refer to the planet Venus, as it turns out, but that fact wasn't always known, and isn't known to everybody. So somebody could hold one set of beliefs about the morning star and another set about the evening star. But then the puzzle is how this is possible: The two are the same, so any fact that holds of one must necessarily hold of the other as well. The sense/reference distinction resolved the problem by taking the **sense** of an expression to be its descriptive meaning, the aspect under which we are presenting the referent. The morning star, then, is the star we see in the morning. The **reference** of an expression, on the other hand, is the object this sense picks out in the world. Therefore, it's possible for a single **referent** to be referred to under different senses, as in the morning star/evening star case or the chickpea/garbanzo bean case. And this isn't a case of cognitivism vs. referentialism, because, on Frege's theory, it's not a question of whether the referent is in the speaker's head or in the world: The referent is always something in the world.

This solves the puzzle posed by (12) above: A sentence like *George believes garbanzo beans are delicious* is essentially ambiguous between a 'sense' reading and a 'reference' reading for the phrase *garbanzo beans*. That is, there are two meanings for this sentence, described in (13):

(13) a   Regarding the real-world objects that are garbanzo beans, George believes them to be delicious.

   b   George has a set of beliefs attached to the term *garbanzo beans*, and one of these beliefs is that they are delicious.

Sentence (12) is true on the reading in (13a): George has tasted the things that are denoted by – which is to say, the things that are the referent of – the term *garbanzo beans*, and he believes they're delicious. However, sentence (12) is false on the reading in (13b): The sense that George has assigned to the term *garbanzo beans* – the set of descriptive beliefs he has assigned to that term – does not include the idea that they are delicious.

We say that a verb like *believe* is a **propositional-attitude** verb, because it expresses someone's attitude about a proposition (here, whether or not they believe it). Propositional-attitude verbs are interesting because they don't allow us to swap out co-referential terms in the embedded sentence that follows them and preserve the truth or falsity of the sentence. Consider, for example, the difference between (14a) and (14b):

(14) a   Garbanzo beans are round.
    b   Chickpeas are round.

Because garbanzo beans and chickpeas are the same thing, if (14a) is true, (14b) is true, and vice versa. It cannot be the case that garbanzo beans have one shape and chickpeas have another. Co-referential terms are terms that have the same referent, and in general when you swap in one for the other, the truth or falsity of the sentence is preserved:

(15) a   The morning star is actually a planet.
    b   The evening star is actually a planet.
    c   Venus is actually a planet.

If any one of these is true, they are all true, and if any one of these is false, they are all false. Similarly:

(16) a   Black-eyed Susan petals are yellow.
    b   *Rudbeckia hirta* petals are yellow.

Again, since *black-eyed Susans* and *Rudbeckia hirta* have the same referent, what's true of one is true of the other. But for all of these examples, if you embed the sentence within a larger sentence, immediately following a propositional-attitude verb, all bets are off:

(17) a   Celia believes that garbanzo beans are round.
    b   Celia believes that chickpeas are round.
    c   Celia believes that the morning star is actually a planet.
    d   Celia believes that the evening star is actually a planet.
    e   Celia believes that black-eyed Susan petals are yellow.
    f   Celia believes that *Rudbeckia hirta* petals are yellow.

Here, it's entirely possible for (a) to be true while (b) is false, and similarly for pairs (c)–(d) and (e)–(f). This is because there's a reading for each of these sentences under which we're not talking about the referents of these expressions at all, but rather the **sense** of the expression, its descriptive meaning.

Keep in mind, though, that each of the sentences in (17) is still ambiguous; there's a less commonly intended, but still available, reading in which each one does refer to the real-world object. So Celia may adamantly insist that black-eyed Susans have white petals, but as long as she's seen (and remembers having seen) the flowers that the rest of us call black-eyed Susans – and assuming she's recognized their petals as being yellow (i.e., she wasn't misled by a trick of the light, she's not profoundly color-blind, etc.), we could say of (17e) that it's true on this alternate reading – the reading under which for the things that are actually black-eyed Susans, she believes that their petals are yellow. We'll have more to say about this in Chapter 3, when we talk about referential opacity.

Referential vs. attributive meaning

So far we've seen two uses of the word *referential* or *reference* in comparison to an alternative: the distinction between a cognitivist and a referentialist view of meaning, and the distinction between sense and reference. In the first case, we asked whether a referring expression actually refers to an object outside of the speaker's mind (the referentialist view) or to a construct in a speaker's set of beliefs (the cognitivist view). In the second case, we looked at a related but distinct ambiguity between the generally accepted linguistic meaning of an expression (its sense) and what that sense picks out in the world (its reference).

Ah, you say; this is finally clear. We've got closely related but distinct uses of an annoyingly similar set of terms (referentialist/referent/reference), but it can all be teased apart into some useful and ultimately clear distinctions. And the last thing on earth you want to hear is that there's one more distinction that makes use of the word *referential.* Unfortunately, philosopher Keith Donnellan (1966) has given us the highly intuitive distinction between a **referential** and an **attributive** use of a referring expression.

Consider Donnellan's famous example in (18):

(18) Smith's murderer is insane.

Imagine the following scenario: You, as a detective, are called in to a crime scene, where you find Smith's body. He has been horribly murdered. Due to the gruesome nature of the crime, and without knowing who committed it, you utter (18). In this case, what you mean is that whoever murdered Smith, that person is clearly insane.

Now imagine a different scenario: You're a detective called to the crime scene. You've been told in advance that Jones murdered Smith, and based on your previous knowledge of Jones's crimes, you believe Jones to be insane. One of the police officers already on the scene asks whether you know why the crime was committed, and you utter (18). In this case, what you mean isn't that whoever murdered Smith is insane; it's that Jones is insane. This reading 'feels' quite different from the above reading.

Donnellan called the first reading the attributive reading: You are using a particular attribute – in this case, that of being Smith's murderer – to pick out an individual, and whatever individual is picked out by that attribute, that's who you're talking about; that's the person you're saying is insane, whether or not you know who it is. He called the second reading the referential reading: You have a specific person in mind to whom you intend to refer, and you're using the referring expression for that purpose.

According to Donnellan, the difference is in what happens if you're wrong about the identity of Smith's murderer. So let's return to poor Smith. Suppose, in the second scenario, you've been wrongly informed: Jones isn't actually the murderer. You're still right about Jones being insane; it's just that Jones had nothing to do with Smith's murder. According to Donnellan, in this case when you utter (18) you've still said something true; that is, you've said something true of Jones, who is in fact insane. You just happened to be wrong about the referring expression you used to pick out Jones.

This is similar to the above question regarding the glass that's believed to hold water but actually holds vodka: Donnellan would say that *The woman holding a glass of water is my mother* is true on the referential reading as long as the intended woman is the speaker's mother, regardless of what's in her glass.

On the attributive reading, in contrast, no such 'rightness' or 'truth' is possible in the face of an inaccuracy of the referring expression: On the attributive reading, (18) is true if and only if **whoever** murdered Smith is insane.

On the one hand, this distinction seems clear, and it accords with our intuitions that these are very different readings of *Smith's murderer.* But on closer inspection, difficulties emerge. First, suppose that despite the gruesome crime scene, Smith is actually still alive, revives, and ends up being just fine with a little medical care. But you uttered (18) with an attributive reading under the sincere belief that Smith was dead. The problem is that although (18) here still permits an attributive reading ('whoever did this is insane'), it seems just as capable of being true of an inaccurately described assailant as in the situation described in the last paragraph. That is, in the situation described there, we had Jones inaccurately described as *Smith's murderer*, and (according to Donnellan) you were able to truthfully predicate insanity of Jones under the referential reading, despite being inaccurate in the expression you used to refer to Jones. Similarly, if you wrongly believe that Smith has died, you can truthfully predicate insanity of the assailant under the attributive reading, despite being inaccurate in the expression you used to refer to this assailant by uttering (18). In short, truth in the face of an inaccurate referring expression doesn't actually distinguish the two readings.

Finally, the strong intuition concerning the two distinct readings becomes much fuzzier in contexts where the referent isn't a human. Suppose poor luckless Smith is walking downtown and a cement block falls off a crumbling old building as he walks past, flattening him. You as the detective arriving on the scene utter (19):

(19) The block that fell on this man killed him instantly.

Can you easily distinguish between a referential and an attributive reading for this sentence? It's a much trickier intuition, in part because in the initial scenario for (18), the difference hinged on whether you knew 'who' the murderer was. In the case of a person, that makes sense – but it makes somewhat less sense in the case of a cement block, because the only important property that distinguishes this block from any other one is that of having fallen on Smith. So it's hard to think in terms of an attributive reading, where what you mean is 'whichever block it was'. The intuition is that we know which block it was; it's the one that killed Smith. Even if, by the time you arrive, the block has been removed from the scene and you're unable to see the spot it fell from, it doesn't matter; for all relevant purposes, you know exactly 'which' block it was.

What makes the difference in the case of a human being is that there are so many other properties that distinguish one human from another in our minds that there's a lot more that goes into our sense of knowing 'who' someone is. So consider the examples in (20):

(20) a   Do you know who that cellist is?
     b   Do you know who Yo-Yo Ma is?

Presumably you could answer (20a) with *Yes, that's Yo-Yo Ma*; in this case, it seems that knowing the referent's name counts as knowing 'who' he is. But you could equally well answer (20b) with *Yes, he's a cellist*; in this case, it seems that knowing a salient property about him counts as knowing 'who' he is. And you needn't even know he plays the cello. Suppose you're lucky enough to be attending a cocktail party for famous musicians; even if all you know about Yo-Yo Ma is his name and his appearance, you could give either of the following responses:

(21) A: Do you know who that guy over there is?
     B: Yes, that's Yo-Yo Ma.
(22) A: Do you know who Yo-Yo Ma is?
     B: Yeah, he's that guy over there.

So it seems rather complicated to say what it is to know someone's identity; it depends in part on what pieces of information you already have about them, and what you still lack. In (18) under the referential reading, what gives you (in your guise as our detective) the knowledge of 'who' killed Smith is that you have other information about this person – their name, for example. In the cement-block case in (19), it's much harder to imagine any other information that could render one block distinguishable from any other besides the property mentioned in the referring expression. And for that reason, the distinction between a referential and an attributive reading vanishes.

In short, then, while there is an intuitive sense of an expression being 'referential' if you can pick out its referent based on some property **other** than the one mentioned in the referring expression (where the referring expression is, e.g., *Smith's murderer*), and 'attributive' if that's the only property you know of, in another sense all referring expressions are equally referential by virtue of being referring expressions. That is, regardless of what you know of Smith's murderer in (18) beyond the property of having murdered Smith, you've still got a mental referent for this entity.

Possible worlds and discourse models

Having become comfortable with the notion of 'mental referents' – or entities that exist somehow in the speaker's head as opposed to in the real world (though presumably most of these correspond to entities that exist in the real world as well), you may be wondering exactly where in the speaker's head we'll find all these entities. In order to work our way toward answering that question, let's first return to what we've been treating as the alternative locale for referents to reside in: the real world.

Let's say, for the sake of argument, that a reality exists outside of the language user's mind. That seems pretty uncontroversial. We can probably all agree that we live in some reality that is genuine, actual, that really truly exists; choose your favorite term. But as we've seen in many examples above, from chickpeas to cellists, we can be wrong about the details of the real world, and of course no one knows everything about that world. This has raised interesting questions about what precisely we're talking about when we talk about something that we **think** exists in the real world but doesn't, or when we refer to something in the real world in terms of a property we believe it to possess that it in fact doesn't (which in turn raises questions about what the 'it' is that we believe we've referred to).

But another interesting fact is that each of these misconceptions about the nature of the real world constitutes a way that the world **might** have been, but just happens not to be. And in fact, there are an infinite number of ways in which the world could have turned out to be different from what it's actually like. For example, yesterday I went grocery shopping – but I could instead have decided not to go grocery shopping. And had I made that decision, the subsequent nature of the world would have been changed in innumerable (and probably not very important) ways: I might have run out of orange juice this morning, I'd have several fewer items in my refrigerator right now, I wouldn't have had Italian bread with dinner last night and consequently might weigh very slightly less than I do now, etc.

Philosophers and physicists alike have debated the extent to which a decision (like my decision to shop) is predetermined by earlier events, and how much of an effect tiny differences in the world (like my having bread last night, or – more classically – an extra flutter of a butterfly's wings) might have on the rest of the world. Fortunately, we can sidestep those arguments, because unless we view the universe as completely deterministic (in which case I never had any choice about shopping at all, and the purchase of that bread was already predetermined millions of years ago), there are an infinite number of logically possible ways that the world could have been, had things turned out differently. And even if reality is completely deterministic, it's still **logically** possible that it could have ended up differently. Each way that the world might have been, including the way it actually is, is called a **possible world**.

Needless to say, there are an infinite number of possible worlds. In one possible world, dogs don't have tails. In another possible world, this book is written by someone else. In another possible world, there's no such thing as gravity, and everything is held to the ground with rubber bands. The laws of physics don't have to hold as we know them – but, importantly, the laws of logic do. So there are possible worlds in which each of the following is true, but no possible world in which they are all true:

(23) a   There are dogs.
      b   All dogs have tails.
      c   No dogs have tails.

A world that's logically contradictory is not a possible world. And for the sake of discussion, we'll also stipulate that the English we use to talk about a possible world is external to that world. So we can say that there's no possible world in which (24) is true:

(24) There are dogs, but none of them are canine.

It's worth noting that we talk about alternative worlds all the time. I can utter any of the following, and you'll be able to make judgements about its truth or falsity:

(25) a   I might buy a new car next week, but I might not.

b   Dorothy killed the Wicked Witch of the West by pouring boiling oil on her.

c   Frodo and Gandalf are identical twins.

You can probably tell me immediately that (25a) is true; although it invokes two distinct alternative worlds, you know that one or the other will end up being true, i.e., that I'll either buy a new car or I won't. On the other hand, you would probably say that (25b) and (25c) are false, because you recognize (in this case, largely because of the names) the fictional worlds I have in mind, and you know the basic outlines of those worlds as their authors conceived of them. Each of these fictional worlds is a possible world, although neither of them is a real world in the sense that the characters in question are actual physical beings carrying out the activities of killing wicked witches or dropping rings into volcanoes (to the best of my knowledge). Nonetheless, we carry around a model of each of these worlds in our heads: We know that Dorothy traveled with her dog Toto from Kansas to Oz, had a series of adventures that involved befriending several interesting characters, and ultimately returned safely home to Kansas. We have a **discourse model** that allows us to talk with each other about this world.

Of course, our discourse models for this world are likely to differ. Indeed, if you read the L. Frank Baum book *The Wonderful Wizard of Oz* but never saw the movie *The Wizard of Oz*, whereas I saw the movie but never read the book, our discourse models for this world are likely to be very different, reflecting the differences between the book and the film. Thus, discourse models aren't truly shared, although researchers often talk as though they are.

This should remind you of Reddy's arguments against the Conduit Metaphor, where we considered the possibility that the vast majority of our communicative efforts are imperfect (despite our seldom becoming aware of that fact) due to the differences in our mental worlds. Briefly stated, it's not only our models of Oz that differ; our models of the real world differ, too. Successful communication assumes a certain amount of overlap between what speakers and hearers take the world in question to be like – that is, their discourse models. Speakers and hearers, in turn, generally assume their worlds are very similar (or, sometimes, argue about the perceived differences). In fact, they make this assumption precisely because they assume they're talking about the real world directly, without stopping to think about the mental representations they have of that world and the question of whether those representations are accurate or not.

So we'll be talking quite a bit in this book about these discourse models. But what is this notion of a 'discourse' that we've been implicitly assuming? For linguists, a **discourse** is a connected series of utterances (spoken or written) that are intended as a coherent sequence, regardless of how many participants there are. A newspaper article is a discourse; so is this book. So is the conversation you had with your roommate over breakfast. Perhaps your roommate told you something interesting that they learned from an article in this morning's newspaper; they now have something in their discourse model that they'd like you to have in yours, so they'll describe it to you, and you can add it to your model, and now you can refer to it in later conversation.

Every discourse assumes a discourse model. Strictly speaking, in fact, it assumes that each participant has a discourse model; interlocutors, meanwhile, operate on the assumption that these discourse models are fundamentally similar (that is, there's a convenient fiction of a shared discourse model). And every discourse model is a mental model of a possible world whose elements can be referred to in a discourse concerning that world. So I can refer to your roommate and the breakfast you had together and the conversation you had because I invented, on the fly, a discourse model in which you (whoever you are) indeed have a roommate and the two of you had a conversation over breakfast on the morning of your reading this. Chances are actually pretty slim that that's an accurate description of your living situation and your morning, but it doesn't matter. I could easily have moved on from that last paragraph without commenting on the unlikelihood of that situation holding in the real world; writers do that sort of thing all the time. And you would have accepted it, understanding that I had invented a nonce discourse model for the sake of making a point and that I didn't have any expectation that it matched reality.

Mostly, though, we tend to discuss the actual world, and we expect that there's a certain match between what is said in the discourse and that world. And generally, to the extent that a statement matches the actual world, we consider it to be true. But truth is always relative to the world under discussion, so when you (presumably) judged (25b) above to be false, it wasn't because you thought there was any actual person named Dorothy in the real world who killed an actual witch with some liquid substance (though it's entirely possible that that did happen, unbeknownst to either of us); rather, you judged it to be false because you recognized the discourse model I had evoked – which in turn describes a particular possible world assumed in the story of the Wizard of Oz – and you realized that you had a similar discourse model (though you probably thought of it as the same discourse model, disregarding the differences I highlighted later) and used that model as the basis for your judgment of the statement's truth.

Okay, so why am I belaboring all of this? It seems as though we've traveled relatively far from our goal of examining meaning, into the realm of truth and the relationship between truth and belief and between the real world and other possible worlds. It all seems pretty philosophical – and it is! – but you would be excused for wondering what it all has to do with meaning. And the answer, in short, is everything. The notion of possible worlds will turn out to be crucial to theories of truth, and the notion of truth will turn out to be crucial to semanticists' theories of meaning. So before leaving philosophy and turning to semantics, let's spend a little time focusing on truth.

Meaning and truth

Assuming that there are an infinite number of possible worlds (though possibly only one **actual** world; physicists are debating that question), there are some things that will be true in a given world and some things that will be false in it. These 'things' are propositions. That is, we define a **proposition** as something that can be either true or false. The sentences in (26) all express the same proposition:

(26) a   Jessie threw a cheesecake into the lake.
     b   A cheesecake was thrown into the lake by Jessie.
     c   Into the lake Jessie threw a cheesecake.

Setting aside Jessie's potential motives for this unusual action, one thing we can say pretty safely is that each of these sentences describes the same situation, and so for any given possible world (involving an agreed-upon set of referents for *Jessie* and *the lake*), if any one of them is true, they're all true, and if any one of them is false, they're all false. So a proposition is distinct from a **sentence**, since all of these sentences are different but they all express the same proposition. It's also worth noting that a sentence, in turn, is distinct from an **utterance**, since all of these were sentences of English a year before I wrote them, but until I wrote them, it's entirely possible that none of them had ever before been uttered. In fact, there are an infinite number of perfectly good English sentences that have not yet been uttered. From this, we can conclude a few basic things:

- An utterance is the use of a given sentence in a particular context (whether spoken, written, or signed).
- A (declarative) sentence is the expression of a proposition in a particular form in a particular language, regardless of whether it's ever actually uttered (although, interestingly, a given sentence can express different propositions on different occasions of utterance, depending, for example, on which lake is being referred to by *the lake*).
- A proposition may be expressed in any number of forms or languages, but it will always be the sort of thing that can be either true or false.

Many semanticists are adherents of **truth-conditional** semantics, a theory in which the meaning of a sentence is the proposition it expresses, which is exactly the same thing as saying that the meaning of a sentence is the set of worlds in which it is true. But wait – it seems as though we've taken quite a leap there, right? It seems pretty reasonable for the meaning of a sentence to be the proposition it expresses, and it seems equally reasonable to say that a proposition can be true or false in a given world. But saying that the meaning of a sentence is itself nothing more than a set of worlds seems counterintuitive. So let me argue for why this notion might make sense.

First, it allows for a certain parallelism between the meaning of a word and the meaning of a sentence. As we'll see in Chapter 3, the meaning of a word can be thought of as a procedure for deciding what it does and doesn't apply to. And that, in turn, corresponds nicely to how children seem to acquire language. A child sees an object and is told that it's a *dog*. And at some point they see another object which is also a *dog*. And so forth, and over time they develop a sense of what counts as a *dog*. They'll have some set of features that constitute, in their mind, dog-ness, which may include such factors as appearance, size, behavior, and treatment (dogs are kept as pets, while coyotes and wolves are not), and there will also be features to distinguish dogs from cats, horses, goldfish, etc. So the question of what is a dog is really the question of what it takes for a given object to count as a dog. The word *dog* **denotes** (roughly speaking, 'picks out') a particular set of individual objects.

Now consider a sentence. Rather than picking out a set of individual objects, a sentence picks out a set of situations involving the denotations of the words in the sentence. So *Jessie threw a cheesecake into the lake* denotes a set of scenarios in which a person we are calling Jessie threw a cheesecake into a particular lake. And just as the meaning of the word *dog* represents a decision procedure for determining whether the word *dog* does or doesn't accurately describe a particular object, the meaning of the sentence *Jessie threw a cheesecake into the lake* represents a decision procedure for determining whether this sentence does or doesn't accurately describe a particular scenario – which is the same as saying that it corresponds to the question of whether that sentence is true in a given world. Thus, the meaning of a sentence ends up corresponding precisely to the set of worlds in which it is true. The set of worlds in which it is true, in turn, corresponds precisely to the set of conditions under which it is true (which is just another way of saying 'the worlds in which it is true'), and for this reason the theory is known as **truth-conditional semantics**. The conditions under which a sentence is true are (not surprisingly) its **truth-conditions**. The truth-conditions are to be distinguished from a sentence's **truth-value** in a given world, which is simply whether it is true or false in that world. For any sentence, its truth-conditions are absolute – they don't vary from world to world – whereas its truth-value is relative to a given world, such that in some worlds it will be true and in some it will be false.

This approach isn't without its difficulties, as we'll see later, but it has proven extremely useful. Early semanticists took from the study of logic the notion that the meanings of some very basic words could be usefully represented in terms of truth. The simplest of these words is *not*, which simply reverses the truth-value of a given proposition with respect to a given world – which, in turn, is just a fancy way of saying that if *Jessie threw a cheesecake into the lake* is true, then *Jessie did not throw a cheesecake into the lake* is false. Because the 'meaning' of the word *not* is a function it performs on the truth of a proposition (i.e., it functions to reverse a proposition's truth-value), it's called a **truth-functional operator**.

Logicians and semanticists have a way of showing how a truth-functional operator affects a proposition: the **truth table**. The truth-functional operator known as **negation** (exemplified by the word *not*) has the truth table shown in Table 2.1.

Table 2.1 Negation

p	$\neg p$
t	f
f	t

Here's how you read it: p stands for any proposition (such as *Jessie threw a cheesecake into the lake* or *Cheesecake floats* or *The Cubs won the 2016 World Series*) – any proposition at all. The symbol '$\neg$' stands for negation (i.e., *not*). Each horizontal row (after the top one) stands for a set of possible worlds, defined by the truth-value in the left column. So what this table says is that in any world in which p is true (those are the worlds in the first row), $\neg p$ ('*not p*') is false. And in any world in which p is false (those are the worlds in the second row), $\neg p$ is true. Since those exhaust the set of possible worlds, this exhausts the effect of the negation. And intuitively, this does seem to be the meaning of *not*.

There are several other truth-functional operators that are called **logical connectives** because they connect propositions, and their meanings can be specified entirely in terms of the effect they have on the truth of the resulting combination. For example, if we know that the sentence *Jessie threw a cheesecake into the lake* is true in a given world, and we know that the sentence *Cheesecake floats* is true in that same world, then it follows from the meaning of the word *and* that the compound sentence *Jessie threw a cheesecake into the lake, and cheesecake floats* is necessarily true in that same world. That is, the semantic meaning of *and* as a sentence connective is no more and no less than the fact that if both of the sentences it conjoins are true, the resulting conjoined sentence is true, and if either of them is false, the resulting conjoined sentence is false. The truth table for **conjunction** (i.e., *and*) is shown in Table 2.2.

Table 2.2 Conjunction

p	q	$p \wedge q$
t	t	t
t	f	f
f	t	f
f	f	f

Here, we've introduced a new proposition: q. The italicized p and q are called **variables** because what they stand for can vary; it can be any proposition at all. Again, the rows exhaust the possible worlds, but because we've got two variables, we'll need twice as many rows – one for each possible combination of truth and falsity for our two propositions. So there are possible worlds where p and q are both true, and there are worlds where p is true but q is false, and there are worlds where p is false and q is true, and finally there are worlds where both p and q are false. But – no matter what propositions p and q stand for – there are no other possible worlds.

As expected, Table 2.2 shows that if p is true and q is true in a given world, then $p \wedge q$ (where '$\wedge$' stands for *and*) is true. If either of them is false, or if both of them are false, then $p \wedge q$ is also false.

The truth table for *or* is slightly less obvious. Whereas we use the term **conjunction** for cases where two sentences are joined by *and*, we use the word **disjunction** for cases where two sentences are joined by *or*. Nonetheless, *or* is another logical connective, because its semantic meaning (like that of *and*) is a function performed on two sentences based on their truth-values. The truth table is shown in Table 2.3.

Table 2.3 Disjunction

p	q	$p \vee q$
t	t	t
t	f	t
f	t	t
f	f	f

Here, the symbol '∨' stands for *or*. (Be sure not to confuse it with '∧', which stands for *and*.) The last three rows make intuitive sense: If one of the two propositions is true and the other is false, it makes sense that $p \vee q$ ('p or q') is true; if both are false, then of course $p \vee q$ is false. You might feel a twinge of uncertainty about the first row, where p and q are both true, because we often use the word *or* in what's called an 'exclusive' way: If I tell you that you may have cheesecake or apple pie for dessert, you will often assume that having them both isn't an option. This reading is called **exclusive *or***. If we were to create a truth table for exclusive *or*, it would look like the one in Table 2.3 except that in the top row, $p \vee q$ would be listed as false, because on that reading if p and q are both true, then $p \vee q$ is false.

So why do we show $p \vee q$ as true in the first row of Table 2.3? One reason is that in lots of other situations, we wouldn't want to say that if p and q are both true, then $p \vee q$ is false. Consider a situation in which I've introduced you to Harrison Ford at a party (lucky you!), and, a bit unsure of his film credits, I tell you:

(27) Mr. Ford played Han Solo in *Star Wars* or Indiana Jones in *Raiders of the Lost Ark*.

Now in truth, of course, he played both of these roles. And I'm sure that in our party-introduction scenario, he would gently point this out. But would you want to say that what I've said in (27) is false? Would it make more sense for him to respond with (28a) or (28b)?

(28) a You're right; I played both roles.
     b You're wrong; I played both roles.

The standard assumption among logicians and semanticists is that (27) is true (in the current world), and that (28a) is a more reasonable response. And suppose I tell a child (29):

(29) For your birthday, I'm going to give you either a bicycle or a wagon.

If I give the child both a bicycle and a wagon, are they entitled to feel that I lied? Again, the standard assumption is no, I've told the truth – which means that the first row of Table 2.3 is correct.

Why, then, do we so often assume that someone who says $p \lor q$ intends to also convey $\neg(p \land q)$? That is to say, why is it that someone who says 'p or q' is taken to mean not only 'p or q' but also 'it's not the case that both p and q'? As it happens, that's one of the questions that helped to give rise to the modern field of pragmatics, which addresses the difference between what we've said semantically and what we meant in saying it. Philosopher H.P. Grice argued that semantically, *or* means just exactly what's shown in Table 2.3 as the truth table for **inclusive *or*** – which is the 'logical' *or* that logicians use. Our assumption that the use of *p or q* in a given case excludes the possibility that *p* and *q* are both true comes from a practical, 'pragmatic' consideration, which is that if the speaker knew both *p* and *q* to be true, they should have said *p and q* rather than *p or q*: Choosing the less informative *p or q* in that situation is just unhelpful. That is, if I know that Harrison Ford played both of the roles listed in (27), it's unhelpful and border-line perverse to utter (27), and my hearer knows it. So the hearer will figure that I'm in no position to say that Ford played both roles. In Chapter 4, we'll consider this distinction between the semantic and pragmatic uses of *or* in more detail, and we'll discuss Grice's ground-breaking principle offering a mechanism for the hearer's inference to exclusivity in the meaning of *or*. For now, we'll continue to take the inclusive meaning as the semantic meaning of *or*, with the exclusive meaning being derived via pragmatic principles.

Now we come to our third connective, which is called **material implication**, or the **conditional**, and is indicated by the symbol '$\rightarrow$'. In English, material implication is often expressed as *if p, then q*, or more formally as *p implies q*. The truth table is, again, initially coun-terintuitive, as shown in Table 2.4.

Table 2.4 Conditional

p	q	$p \rightarrow q$
t	t	t
t	f	f
f	t	t
f	f	t

Here, the first line says that if *p* and *q* are true, then it's true that 'if *p*, then *q*'. That makes sense, and it also makes sense that when *p* is true and q is false, it's certainly not the case that 'if p, then q'. So the second row is also intuitively correct. The third row is trickier; it says that if p is false and q is true, then *if p, then q* is true. And the fourth row seems equally odd; it says that if p and q are both false, then *if p, then q* is true. How does that make sense?

Here it may help to use the 'lie' test: Suppose I've told you (30):

(30) If it snows tomorrow, I'll take you sledding.

The first two rows of Table 2.4 address the possible worlds in which it snows tomorrow. In the first row, it snows (i.e., p is true), and I take you sledding (q is true), and all is well; I've clearly spoken the truth, and $p{\rightarrow}q$ is true. In the second row, it snows, and I don't take you sledding; here I've clearly lied, and my utterance in (30), of the form $p{\rightarrow}q$, is false. Now, what if it doesn't snow? The last two rows address this question. In the third row, it doesn't snow, and I take you sledding anyway. (Maybe in this case there's snow on the ground from a previous snowfall.) Is my utterance in (30) a lie? It's hard to imagine anybody saying it is; after all, my statement in (30) says nothing at all about whether I'll take you sledding if it doesn't snow. And the fourth row represents a world in which it doesn't snow and I don't take you sledding, and certainly in this world I haven't lied either. The material implication is really only about worlds in which p is true; if p is false, then all bets are off, and $p{\rightarrow}q$ cannot possibly be false (which is why it's judged true in both of the last two rows).

You can see here how these truth tables mesh with our view of 'truth' as being relative to a possible world, and specifically the view that the meaning of a proposition corresponds to the set of worlds in which it's true; this view is precisely why the last two rows of Table 2.4 make sense. In essence, we're focusing on the worlds in which p is true and then checking to see whether, **in those worlds**, q is also true. The last two rows of Table 2.4 say that $p{\rightarrow}q$ is true whenever it's basically irrelevant (the worlds in which p is false). And here again, the difference between the semantic view of the logical operators and their usual use in natural language is accounted for as a pragmatic phenomenon: When we utter a sentence like (30), our hearer will usually assume there's a causal relationship between p and q (that is, a relationship in which *p* causes *q*), but that's just because there's no reason at all for the speaker to utter the *p* clause (the **antecedent**) if it has nothing to do with the *q* clause (the **consequent**). Since the speaker has gone to the bother of mentioning *p*, the hearer will assume it must be relevant, but logically speaking, this isn't necessary. So in the real world, I could utter (31):

(31) If January immediately precedes February, the U.S. is in North America.

It's hard to imagine a context in which I'd want to say this, because there's no apparent relationship between the order of the months and the location of the U.S. But from a strictly semantic point of view, the antecedent and the consequent in (31) are both true; hence, (31) as a whole is true. And (32) is equally true:

(32) If January immediately follows February, the U.S. is in North America.

This doesn't 'feel' quite right for pragmatic reasons, but if you've followed the argument above, you may be willing to acknowledge that – at least logically – it is in fact true. In any world in which the consequent (the *q* clause) is true, the truth of the antecedent (the *p* clause) is irrelevant: The U.S. is in North America regardless of the ordering of January and February, which is just to say that if *q* is true, then $p{\rightarrow}q$ is true whether *p* is true or not.

The last logical connective we'll address here is the **biconditional**, which corresponds to the English phrase *if and only if*. In fact, logicians use the shorthand *iff* to stand for this phrase. The truth table for the biconditional is given in Table 2.5.

Table 2.5 Biconditional

p	*q*	$p{\leftrightarrow}q$
t	t	t
t	f	f
f	t	f
f	f	t

Here we see that $p \leftrightarrow q$ is true whenever (if and only if!) the truth value of p and q are the same. This makes sense: *p if and only if q* should mean that p is true whenever q is true, and false whenever q is false, and vice versa. So you get exactly the expected results for cases like (33):

(33) You'll get a bike for your birthday if and only if Mom gets a raise.

Here, either Mom gets a raise and the addressee gets a bike, or neither of those things happens. If one happens and the other doesn't, (33) is false. The less intuitive situation, as with the conditional, is when p and q have nothing to do with each other, as in (34):

(34) The Earth has a moon if and only if Chicago is in Illinois.

Now, (34) is true in the current world (where the Earth does in fact have a moon and Chicago is in fact in Illinois), and it would be equally true if neither of those things were the case, but false if one were true and the other false. But it feels a bit odd to see that (34) is true in the current world, because we interpret it as suggesting that there's some causal relationship between these two propositions – that is, that somehow the existence of Earth's moon depends on Chicago being in Illinois. Again, however, this relationship is based on our sense that it's pointless to utter (34) in any context in which the moon's existence doesn't depend on Chicago being in Illinois. Since this is a fact about contextual appropriateness, it's a pragmatic fact, not a semantic one. Semantically, $p \leftrightarrow q$ is true whenever p and q have the same truth-value – which, rather nicely, means that it's true iff p and q have the same truth-value. You could represent this last statement as (35):

(35) $(p \leftrightarrow q) \leftrightarrow ((p \wedge q) \vee (\neg p \wedge \neg q))$

This looks a bit daunting, but if you take it piece by piece, it's easy to read. This simply says: $p \leftrightarrow q$ if and only if it's either the case that $p \wedge q$ or it's the case that $\neg p \wedge \neg q$, i.e., iff either p and q are both true or they're both false.

Notice that parentheses are used to group things together, and how they group things affects the meaning – and truth – of the result. So (36a) and (36b) mean different things, and will be true in different worlds:

(36) a $(p \land q) \to r$
     b $p \land (q \to r)$

Here, (36a) means 'if $p \land q$ is the case, then r is also the case'; (36b), on the other hand, means 'p is the case, and if q is the case, then so is r.' (Notice that we had to move to the next letter of the alphabet in order to bring in a third proposition.) We can use a bigger truth table to check each of the formulas in (36), as shown in Tables 2.6 and 2.7.

Table 2.6 Complex proposition with three variables

p	q	r	$p \land q$	$(p \land q) \to r$
t	t	t	t	t
t	t	f	t	f
t	f	t	f	t
t	f	f	f	t
f	t	t	f	t
f	t	f	f	t
f	f	t	f	t
f	f	f	f	t

Table 2.7 The same variables and connectives, differently grouped

p	q	r	$q \to r$	$p \land (q \to r)$
t	t	t	t	t
t	t	f	f	f
t	f	t	t	t
t	f	f	t	t
f	t	t	t	f
f	t	f	f	f
f	f	t	t	f
f	f	f	t	f

Once again we need to double the number of rows to accommodate an additional proposition, since all the possible worlds from our previous truth table have to show up twice – once with r being true and once with r being false – in order to accommodate all the possible combinations of p, q, and r being true and false. We first calculate the truth-value of what's grouped together inside the parentheses, and with that truth-value in hand, it's straightforward to calculate the truth-value of the whole thing. For example, in row 1 of Table 2.7, we first determine that $q{\to}r$ is true, because q and r are both true in that world. And since $q{\to}r$ is true, and p is also true, the complete formula $p{\wedge}(q{\to}r)$ is true, as shown in the last column. As you can imagine, there's no limit to the length of the formulas you could make truth tables for, to check their truth in every possible world (that is, every possible combination of truth and falsity for all of their propositional variables). The number of rows needed will double with each new variable, so with two variables you need 2^2 rows (i.e., 4), with three variables you need 2^3 rows (i.e., 8), with four variables you need 2^4 rows (i.e., 16), and so on. Adding a second instance of the same variable, as in a formula like $p{\wedge}(q{\to}p)$, doesn't require the same doubling of rows, since the repeated variable (here, p) represents the same proposition throughout and therefore will have the same truth-value throughout. The fact that the two formulas in (36) mean different things is reflected in the fact that they are true in different sets of worlds, which is seen in the fact that the final columns in these two tables have different sets of t's and f's for the last four rows.

At this point you may feel a bit exhausted, and possibly even a bit cheated: What on earth do all of these tables have to do with language and meaning? We don't talk in p's and q's, after all (even if children were once told to 'mind your p's and q's'). We've shed a tiny bit of light on the meanings of some tiny functional words like *and* and *or* – but even here, in cases where the logical meanings of the connectives differ from their usual use in common language, we've given a bit of a promissory note, saying that their interpretation in daily conversation depends in part on pragmatics, not just on their logical meaning. But as we'll see in the chapters to come, the logical meaning is the basis for these higher-level inferences about the speakers' intent, which is what the 'common use' of these terms really boils down to. So hang in there as we move from these fairly abstract notions to their application in semantics and pragmatics.

Chapter 3

Semantics

The philosophical tradition has been fundamental to what's called **truth-conditional semantics**. Just as the philosophical approach traced in the previous chapter views the meaning of a proposition as the set of worlds in which that proposition is true, truth-conditional semantics views the meaning of a sentence as the set of worlds in which the proposition it expresses is true. This is why different sentences that express the same proposition (for example, an active sentence and its passive variant) will have the same truth-conditions and therefore the same semantic meaning. And as we noted in the previous chapter, just as the meaning of a sentence can be viewed as the set of worlds in which it is true, the meaning of a word can be viewed as the contribution it makes to the truth-conditions of a sentence; thus, the meaning of a referential term can be seen as the set of objects it truthfully describes, the meaning of a logical connective can be seen as the effect it has on the truth of the sentence containing it, and the meaning of an adjective or intransitive verb can be seen as the set of referents of which it truthfully holds. To go into more detail, let's begin with what will seem like a fairly straightforward question.

What does it take to be a chair?

There are words that are so commonly used that it would seem to be self-evident that we all know their meaning. To take a simple example, consider the word *chair*. We all know what the word *chair* means, right? But take it from me – as someone who has raised this question in innumerable undergraduate classes – when you ask a roomful of people to clarify precisely what does and doesn't count as a chair, problems arise almost immediately. If we try for a first pass at what it takes to count as a chair, we might decide on the following features:

- a seat
- legs
- a back

At this point someone is likely to object that a chair doesn't need all of these. A seat might seem necessary – but what about a bean bag chair? Does it have a seat? It doesn't have legs, and there are swivel rockers that have a circular base rather than legs. And what about a back? Is a stool a chair? And what about a couch? Or a bench? Perhaps we should specify that a chair accommodates only one person. But that leaves out love seats, which are designed for two. It turns out that people disagree on whether bean bag chairs, swivel rockers, stools, couches, and benches count as chairs – as well as whether it's necessary for a chair to have a seat, four legs, or a back.

And it's not just the word *chair* that's a problem. The question of what constitutes a *sandwich* went before a Massachusetts judge in 2006. The problem was that a Panera sandwich shop located in a strip mall had a clause in its lease stating that the mall would not lease space to any other sandwich shop. But then they allowed a Qdoba outlet to open in the mall. Qdoba sells burritos; hence, Panera viewed this as a violation of the clause forbidding another sandwich shop. Is a burrito a sandwich? The judge said no. But it's an interesting question: What set of objects does the word *sandwich* properly denote? Is a wrap a sandwich? How about a gyro? A hamburger? A hot dog? A sloppy joe? Some people feel that a hamburger and a sloppy joe are sandwiches, but a hot dog is not. A 2015 article in *The Atlantic* argued that the difference lies in its orientation: A hot dog is vertical, while a hamburger is horizontal. But an Italian beef is generally considered a sandwich, and its orientation is vertical. You might feel tempted to resolve the problem by letting in hot dogs and gyros and even wraps, and declaring a sandwich to be any instance of a filling surrounded on at least two sides by a form of bread. But then what happens to the open-face sandwich? What makes it more of a sandwich than, say, a pizza is? And is a calzone a pizza, a sandwich, or something else?

This all boils down to the question of what features are required for something to count as a sandwich – which is the approach taken by **componential semantics**. In this view, the meaning of a term can be seen as a set of primitive features that an object either must have or must not have in order to count as an instance of that term. So, for example, the word *child* might be:

+human
–adult

That is, a child is a human who is not an adult. And *girl* would then be:

+human
–adult
+female

And *boy* would be:

+human
–adult
–female

And so on. But as we've seen, this system flounders on words as straightforward as *chair* and *sandwich.* In fact, *sandwich* presumably has as its primary requirement:

+bread

But here we encounter the unavoidable question: What counts as bread? Does a pita count as bread? How about a tortilla? Obviously this latter question is crucial to the determination of whether a burrito is a sandwich. And the only thing that's clear is that neither is clear.

Actually, what **is** clear is that people who speak the same language may not agree fully on the meanings of pretty basic words, but since we so rarely need to agree on those borderline cases, communication sails along reasonably smoothly. The fact is, we're never really taught the meanings of basic words in our native language the way we're (usually) taught the meanings of such words in a foreign language. Children encounter a variety of objects that the adults around them label *chair*, and based on that input, they develop a concept of what does and doesn't count as a chair. And since each child encounters a slightly different range of objects that will or won't be labeled *chair*, it's natural that we all develop very slightly different notions of what a term denotes. It's also natural that any given individual will be a bit unclear as to where the range of *chair* stops and the range of *not-a-chair* begins. Or, to be more accurate, there is likely to be a certain number of uncertain cases – cases that the individual might label *kind of a chair* or *chair-like*. That is, there are cases that a speaker will **hedge**, using **hedge words** like *kind of*, *sort of*, *somewhat*, or the suffix *-ish* (as in *chair-ish*).

So if I'm not sure what is and isn't a chair, and you're not sure what is and isn't a chair, and we don't always agree on what is and isn't a chair, how do we manage to communicate using the word *chair* at all? Fortunately, we share a core meaning for *chair*, which is to say, speakers of English pretty much agree on what counts as the most 'chair-like' chair (though this could in principle vary from culture to culture). The most chair-like chair has four legs, a seat, and a back, is intended for sitting, and is designed for occupancy by one person at a time. This is the **prototypical** chair, and the more similar to this **prototype** an object is, the more chair-like it is, and the more properly the word *chair* applies to it. Conversely, the more unlike this prototype an object is, the less chair-like it is. The definition of the word *chair*, then, is 'fuzzy' around the edges, where there will be some objects whose membership in the category denoted by *chair* is 'fuzzy' or uncertain. You can think of a word as denoting a **fuzzy set** shaped like a target, with the prototype being at the bull's-eye or center, other members being distributed at points more or less distant from this target depending on how similar they are to the prototype, other objects whose membership is unclear being at the ill-defined fuzzy edge of the set, and of course an infinite number of other objects being outside the set altogether (the word *chair* simply doesn't apply to a refrigerator).

To return to the word *sandwich*, then, we can safely say that, at least in most American cultures, the prototypical sandwich consists of two thin, flat, horizontal slices of leavened bread surrounding one or more items of filling – typically including lunchmeat, cheese, or peanut butter and jelly. Less central members of the set include sub sandwiches, Italian beef sandwiches, and open-faced sandwiches. Even farther from the center are hamburgers and sloppy joes. And in that fuzzy area that shades into non-sandwich territory we'll find hot dogs, wraps, tacos, burritos, and calzones.

This approach to word meaning is often referred to as **Prototype Theory** due to its reliance on a prototypical member of the set. It is essentially the linguistic version of a more broadly applied theory called **Fuzzy Set Theory**, which in turn uses **fuzzy logic** in applications ranging from mass-transit design to artificial intelligence. The idea in fuzzy logic, as in the Prototype Theory version I've been describing, is to replace the 'crisp' true/false values of classical set theory (either something is in the set or it isn't) with 'fuzzy' values, where set membership, truth-values, and judgments of accuracy/inaccuracy are all matters of degree. The use of this approach in artificial intelligence – especially where artificial intelligence and linguistics intersect – is that, just as a child acquiring a new word is able to refine their understanding of the word each time they encounter it, the machine can likewise refine its 'understanding' of the word each time it encounters it by using these encounters to continually refine the prototype. It's essentially a numerical task, which computers excel at: On the assumption that the vast majority of sandwiches are similar to the prototype, while many fewer are far from the prototype (after all, that's what makes it the prototype), we would expect that statistically, the more instances of the word *sandwich* a computer encounters, the more data it will have for what a prototypical sandwich is like. In this sense, what the computer does in fuzzy-logic-based artificial intelligence tasks is quite similar to what a child does in learning a word.

Relationships between words

One way to think about the meanings of words is by considering how they relate to other words. In knowing a word, we don't know simply what that word itself means; we also know what other words have similar meanings, which ones are opposites, which are used in similar contexts, and so on. To what extent this sort of information is part of the meaning of the word is an interesting question. It seems likely that the meaning of the word *female* is a necessary component of the word *mare*, for instance, as is the meaning of the word *horse*; but what about the meaning of *stallion*? Or *colt*? Does knowing the meaning of *mare* entail knowing its relationship to either of those meanings? If it seems to you that the answer is clearly 'no', then consider whether the meaning of the word *dessert* includes the meaning of the word *sweet.* Is a dessert necessarily sweet? Is it possible that all desserts are sweet but sweetness is not part of the meaning of the word *dessert*? And if both of those cases seem clear to you, do you think knowing the word *house* requires knowing that it's a structure? If it does, does it require knowing the actual word *structure* and the relationship between those two words? If not, then why should knowing the meaning of *dessert* require knowledge that desserts are sweet?

This, of course, to some extent conflates the meaning of a word with the word itself; you can know that desserts have a certain characteristic flavor without knowing that the word *sweet* describes that flavor. But it is also clearly the case that our knowledge of word meanings constitutes a complex network of interconnected meanings: If I choose to describe a certain olfactory stimulus using the word *aroma*, I have rejected a range of alternative options including *scent, odor, smell, fragrance,* and *stench.* And in many cases the available options that I've rejected help to nail down my precise meaning; as we'll see in our discussion of pragmatics, if a recipe says that you should dissolve yeast in *warm* water, the choice of the word *warm* over the alternative option *hot* will itself tend to convey that hot water is not wanted – even though hot water is, strictly speaking, warm.

There are many ways in which words can be related. Among the relations we'll consider are what linguists sometimes think of as the 'nyms' – synonymy, antonymy, hyponymy, and homonymy – along with ambiguity, redundancy, anomaly, polysemy, metonymy, and a smattering of related concepts. And lest you fear this is just an exercise in unnecessary terminology (which, I confess, many academic fields are guilty of, including linguistics), keep in mind that each term corresponds to a distinct aspect of meaning, or a slightly different way in which two words can be related semantically. At the end of the day, it's these properties and relationships that really matter, not the terms we use to describe them.

Perhaps the most familiar of these relations is **synonymy** – that is, the relation of being **synonyms**. (For all of the 'nym' terms, the term referring to the words themselves ends in -*nym*, and the term referring to the general phenomenon ends in -*nymy*.) Synonyms are words that have the same, or very close to the same, meaning, like *pail* and *bucket* or *street* and *road*. Some scholars have argued that there are no true synonyms, since language users tend to avoid developing redundancy in the lexicon. Thus, a pair of terms will show either a difference in dialect or register (as with *couch* and *sofa*) or slight differences in meaning (as with *pail* and *bucket*, where the latter tends to be used for larger containers) or differences in collocation (that is, the words they co-occur with, as with *big* and *large*, where your big brother is not the same as your large brother). The general idea is that if two words truly served identical functions, one of them would die out, since the need to learn and remember two words for the same thing puts an unnecessary burden on the language user with no corresponding payoff.

On the flip side of synonymy, in some sense, is **antonymy**, where two words are 'opposites' in one or another respect. But whereas synonyms are as alike as possible, antonyms are not as different as possible: A pair of antonyms are actually quite similar, being of the same lexical category (noun, verb, etc.) and in the same semantic field. But they do indeed 'oppose' each other within that field, in one of several ways. First, they can be **gradable antonyms**, representing opposing ends of a gradient scale. For example, *hot* and *cold* represent opposite ends of the scale of temperature, and *tall* and *short* represent opposite ends of the scale of height. (*Short* does double duty antonymically, as it is also the antonym of *long* on the scale of length.) Because the scale on which gradable antonyms lie is continuous, it's possible to modify them with adverbs like *very*, *somewhat*, *sort of*, etc., or to add the comparative suffix -*er* or the superlative suffix -*est*. So something can be *very hot*, *very long*, *sort of tall*, *somewhat short*, *longer*, *coldest*, and so on. Often one of the pair is the **unmarked** or default case, while the other is **marked**. So, for example, it's usually considered reasonable to ask someone *How tall are you?* but very rude to ask *How short are you?*, because the latter suggests that the person is unusually short. *How tall are you?*, in contrast, is completely neutral in this regard, and is a reasonable question to ask even of someone who is indeed remarkably short. Similarly, *young* and *old* are gradable antonyms (someone can be *very young* or grow *older*), with *old* being the unmarked member: You can reasonably ask someone of any age how old they are, but again, if you ask someone how young they are it will be taken as suggesting that they are unusually young (or as a patronizing way of treating an elderly person).

A second type of antonyms are **complementary antonyms**. Here there's no gradient involved; if A and B are complementary antonyms, then if you're not A, you're B; and if you're not B, you're A (assuming either of them applies at all). So if you're not alive, you're dead; and if you're not dead, you're alive: *dead* and *alive* are complementary antonyms. If you're not one, you're the other (if either applies at all; that is, a paperclip is neither alive nor dead, because the notion of aliveness doesn't apply). The sorts of hedges and comparatives that can be used with gradable antonyms sound odd, or only work metaphorically, with complementary antonyms: If you say someone is more alive than someone else, this can only be understood metaphorically; there aren't varying degrees of aliveness. Complementary antonyms aren't as common as gradable antonyms, partly because people disagree about what is and isn't gradient. There are, for example, those who would argue that someone who is in a coma, or who has suffered brain death, is less alive than they were previously. Other traditional candidates for complementary antonyms are the pairs *true/false* and *male/female*; but one could argue that there are degrees of truth (for example, is the statement *John is tall* more true if John is seven feet tall than if he is six feet tall?), and society has come to realize that gender is not the binary category it was once taken to be.

The third generally acknowledged category of antonyms is **relational antonyms**, in which two relationships essentially entail each other: That is, if A stands in Relation 1 to B, then B necessarily stands in Relation 2 to A. One example is *parent/child*: If I am your child, you are necessarily my parent, and if you are my parent, I am necessarily your child. Another such relation is *teacher/student*: If I am your teacher, you are my student, and if you are my student, I am your teacher. This reciprocity extends to certain verb pairs, such as *buy* and *sell*: If I buy something from you, you have sold something to me, and vice versa.

Another way two concepts can be related is that one of them encompasses the other; this is the relation of **hyponymy**. Consider, for example, the pair *tree* and *oak*. We say that *oak* is a hyponym of

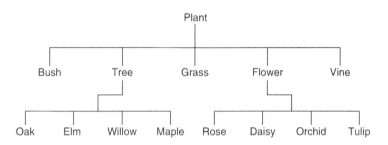

tree. An oak is a tree, which means that the meaning of the word *oak* includes all of the meaning of the word *tree*. (For this reason, hyponymy is often defined as 'meaning inclusion'.) The relationship is also sometimes called an 'isa' relationship: A oak 'is a' type of tree. And speaking of trees, what's called a 'tree diagram' can show a set of such relationships, as shown above.

Now, on the one hand, I'm no botanist, and if I were I'd probably produce a vastly different taxonomy of plants. On the other hand, it doesn't matter; what linguists are interested in is a native speaker's use and understanding of language, and this is a reasonable representation of my use and understanding of plant terms. Obviously I know far more types of flowers than can fit on a page, so this is necessarily partial, but it accurately represents my layperson's understanding that oaks, elms, willows, and maples are all trees; that roses, daisies, orchids, and tulips are all flowers; and that bushes, trees, grasses, flowers, and vines are all plants. If I thought about it very hard, I'd have to acknowledge that flowers are plants in a very different way than vines are plants; for example, a vine can produce flowers, so perhaps a flower is actually a part of a plant (a vine, bush, etc.). But this will work as a rough partial representation of my layperson's knowledge of types of plants. The important thing is that it captures my understanding that for a thing to be a maple, it must also be a tree, and for a thing to be a tree, it must also be a plant. And this relationship is transitive; therefore, for a thing to be a maple, it must also be a plant.

Now, just as we say that *oak* is a hyponym of *tree*, we'd say that *tree* is the superordinate of *oak*. At the same time that it's the superordinate of *oak*, *tree* is also a hyponym of *plant*. And because hyponymy is transitive, if *oak* is a hyponym of *tree* and *tree* is a hyponym of *plant*, *oak* is a hyponym of *plant.* Mutual hyponymy is synonymy: That is, if the meaning of *couch* includes the entire meaning of *sofa* and vice versa, then *couch* and *sofa* mean the same thing and are synonyms.

Hyponymy can give rise to **redundancy**, which is duplication of meaning. If I say *Janet plodded slowly across the road,* I've been redundant, because the word *plod* incorporates the meaning of the word *slowly:* It's impossible to plod quickly across a road. Likewise, it's very odd to say *I sat reading a book under a tree plant.* Once you've said *tree,* it's unnecessary to say *plant,* because the meaning of *tree* incorporates the meaning *plant.* It's the same reason that it's odd to refer to someone as your *female aunt;* the word *aunt* is sufficient. The odd thing is that we do in fact use expressions like *elm tree, oak tree, willow tree,* and *maple tree,* probably more than we use the briefer and equally informative *elm, oak, willow,* and *maple.* An expression like *oak tree* is, strictly speaking, redundant; it's curious that we speak of *oak trees* but rarely of *daisy flowers* – the word *daisy* being quite sufficient.

Whereas two different forms with the same meaning are synonyms, two identical forms with different meanings are **homonyms**. Pairs of homonyms include the *bark* of a dog vs. the *bark* of a tree, *light* meaning 'not dark' vs. *light* meaning 'not heavy', and *bowl* meaning 'a shallow container' vs. *bowl* meaning 'to throw a bowling ball at a set of pins'. Homonyms (*homo* meaning 'same' and *nym* meaning 'name') can give rise to **ambiguity**, which is when a given form has more than one distinct meaning. So a *light marker* can be a marker that is either light in color or light in weight – or, for that matter, something that marks the location of a lamp. And a *light marker* can, therefore, also be a dark marker; I myself own quite a few light dark markers.

We're often taught in grade school that pairs like *light* ('not dark') and *light* ('not heavy') are called **homophones**. Since *homophone* etymologically means 'same sound' (*homo* meaning 'same' and *phone* meaning 'sound'), this is true: Any pair of words that are homonyms are also homophones. But there are also pairs and triplets of words that are homophones (sharing a sound) but not homonyms (sharing a form) because they're spelled differently. Examples include *there, their,* and *they're; to, too,* and *two; sees, seas,* and *seize; prince* and *prints;* and many more (with the last pair giving rise to the old photography pun 'someday my prints will come'). As you can see, although every set of homonyms also constitute homophones, it is not the case that every set of homophones constitute homonyms.

Rounding out the paradigm is the less often used term **homograph**. Homographs are distinct words that are spelled the same (again, not surprising: *homo* 'same' plus *graph* 'writing'), regardless of whether they are pronounced the same. Sets of words that share a spelling but not a pronunciation include the two words spelled *tear* (rhyming with either *fear* or *fair*), the present and past tenses of *read* (rhyming with *seed* and *said*, respectively), and the two words spelled *wound* (rhyming with either *sound* or *tuned*). Again, every set of homonyms also constitute homographs, but it's not the case that every set of homographs constitute homonyms. Homonyms like *bat* (the baseball implement) and *bat* (the flying mammal) are simultaneously both homophones, by virtue of being pronounced the same, and homographs, by virtue of being spelled the same. This, in turn, means that the word *homonym* is a hyponym of both *homophone* and *homograph*: Homonyms are a type of homophone just as a daisy is a type of flower, and homonyms are likewise a type of homograph.

If that doesn't have your head sufficiently reeling, consider now the related notion of **polysemy**. Whereas homonymy is a case of different words (hence different meanings) with the same form, polysemy is a case of the same word (hence the same form) with different but related meanings. Compare our example of *bat* above, where the baseball bat and the flying-mammal bat are clearly distinct words that just happen to have the same form, with a baseball *diamond* vs. *diamond* the gem and *diamond* the shape. Clearly these three meanings are related; the baseball diamond and the diamond on a piece of jewelry take their name from the shape of a diamond. So despite the meanings of the baseball *diamond* and the gem *diamond* being distinct, you wouldn't quite want to say that they are different words in the way that the two types of *bat* are. So whereas the two types of *bat* are homonymous, the two types of *diamond* are polysemous, representing one word with multiple meanings (*poly* 'many', *sem* 'meaning'). Other examples of polysemous pairs include certain cases of a material and a common object made of that material, such as the material called *glass* and a drinking *glass* or the metal called *nickel* and the coin that used to be made of it; materials and their common uses, such as *water* and to *water* the lawn or *butter* and to *butter* your bread; instances of **metonymy**, where a word comes to stand for something closely related to it, as with a *chair* for sitting and the *chair* of a committee; and instances of **synecdoche**, in which the word for a part of a thing comes to mean the whole thing or vice versa, as with *wheels* being used to refer to a car, the *first floor* of a building meaning more than just that level's bottom surface, and *Washington* being used to refer to a subset of people who work there.

The last meaning relation we should consider is **anomaly**. An **anomalous** sentence is one that involves a clash of meanings among the words it is composed of. One way a sentence can be anomalous is to be a **contradiction**; that is, it can simultaneously express two propositions that cannot both be true, as in (1):

(1) #I am taller than Shaun, and Shaun is taller than I am.

(The symbol # is used here to indicate anomaly.) There is no possible world in which (1) can be true; if I'm taller than Shaun, then Shaun cannot be taller than me.

There are other ways in which a sentence can be anomalous, however. For example, recall from Chapter 1 Noam Chomsky's beautifully anomalous sentence:

(2) #Colorless green ideas sleep furiously.

This sentence is semantically gibberish: Nothing can be both colorless and green, ideas can be neither colorless nor green, and so on. The point Chomsky was making with this sentence is that our semantic knowledge and our syntactic knowledge are distinct: We recognize that (2) is semantically problematic even though it's syntactically flawless; therefore, we must use distinct sets of rules to evaluate semantic well-formedness and syntactic well-formedness. Or to put it more straightforwardly, form and meaning are two completely different things.

Relationships between sentences

Just as one way to think about the meanings of words is through their relations to other words, one way to think about the meanings of sentences is through their relations to other sentences. These are in most cases analogous to the lexical relations we looked at above, but there are fewer such relations at the sentential level; after all, it's hard to imagine what sort of sentence would be a homonym of *I took a walk in the woods yesterday.* But since sentence meanings are built up from word meanings, it will be useful, where possible, to think of sentential relations as analogs of lexical relations, just one level up.

Recall, for example, that mutual hyponymy is synonymy: That is, if two words are hyponyms of each other, then each one's meaning must include all of the meaning included in the other, and therefore they must mean exactly the same thing. The sentence-level analog of hyponymy is **entailment**. A sentence entails another sentence if in every possible world in which the first is true, the second is also true; or, to state it a bit more clearly, if sentence A is true, then sentence B is necessarily also true. This means that A includes all of the meaning of B, as in (3)–(5):

(3) a I drank a glass of water.
    b I consumed a glass of water.
(4) a I ate a small pizza and a garden salad.
    b I ate a small pizza.
(5) a I am taller than Sydney, and Sydney is taller than Albert.
    b I am taller than Albert.

As we see in (3), one way for a sentence to entail another sentence is for the first to contain a hyponym of its counterpart in the second, if the two are otherwise identical. There are, of course, other ways for one sentence to entail another. One is shown in (4), where something that is true of the two members of a conjoined pair is obviously true of each of the individual members. Notice, however, that not all conjoined pairs behave this way. Sometimes what is true of the pair isn't necessarily true of each member of the pair:

(6) a Billy and Bobby are the same height.
    b Billy is the same height.

Here, (6b) seems like an odd thing to say unless the height of some other person or thing has been made salient in the context. It's certainly the case that (6a) entails (7):

(7) Billy is the same height as Bobby.

But of course that's not quite what (6b) says.

In both (3) and (4), it makes sense to say that the first sentence in the pair includes the meaning of the second, since *drink* includes the meaning of *consume* and *A and B* includes the meaning of *A* (at least in most cases). But inclusion of meaning isn't the only way for one sentence to entail another: (5a) entails (5b) in the sense that there's no possible world in which (5a) is true while (5b) is false; yet it doesn't seem quite right to say that the meaning of (5a) includes the meaning of (5b); instead, it's a consequence of the way that transitive relationships work. (There's actually an interesting argument to be had over whether this transitivity is itself a consequence of how heights work or of how morphological comparatives like *taller* work, but we'll set that aside.)

Just as, at the word level, mutual hyponymy is synonymy, at the sentence level mutual entailment is **paraphrase**. If sentence A is necessarily true anytime sentence B is true, and vice versa, they are true in exactly the same set of situations or possible worlds; hence, they mean the same thing, as in the pairs in (8)–(10):

(8) a   Jared threw a ball.
     b   A ball was thrown by Jared.
(9) a   Felicia is taller than Kevin.
     b   Kevin is shorter than Felicia.
(10) a   Charlene ate a falafel sandwich and hummus.
     b   Charlene ate hummus and a falafel sandwich.

In each case, neither member of the pair can be true unless the other is true as well. Thus, in each pair, the two sentences are said to be paraphrases of each other – two different ways of saying the same thing.

And just as hyponymy at the word level gives rise to redundancy, so does entailment at the sentence level, as seen in (11), where the initial question mark indicates questionable acceptability:

(11) a   ?My pet Sammy is a cat animal.
     b   ?I own two cars and a motorcycle, and I own a motorcycle.
     c   ?I swam, moving through the water.

In these three cases the oddness is due to redundancy. In (11a), not only does the hyponymic relationship between *cat* and *animal* – where *cat* is a hyponym of *animal* – result in redundancy within the phrase *cat animal*; the redundancy also percolates up to the sentence level, resulting in a redundant sentence. But just as we saw above that hyponymy at the word level is one source, but not the only source, of entailment at the sentence level, here we see that hyponymy is one source, but not the only source, of redundancy at the sentence level. In (11b), we see another source, which has to do not with the word meanings in the sentence, but rather with the form of the sentence: Since *p and q* entails *q*, the first clause of (11b) entails the second, which in turn results in redundancy. In (11c), swimming entails moving through the water, although there are other ways of moving through the water; thus, the relationship between *swam* and *moving through the water* results in redundancy.

The sentence-level analog of word-level antonymy would perhaps be negation, but here the analogy is imperfect. Recall that we considered three types of antonymy: gradable, complementary, and relational. Sentential negation corresponds to complementary antonymy in the sense that the relationship between a sentence and its negation matches that between a word and its complementary antonym, in that a sentence and its negation cannot simultaneously be true. Consider (12):

(12) a   That claim is true.
      b   That claim is not true.
      c   That claim is false.

Negating (12a), as in (12b), has the same effect as replacing the word *true* with its complementary antonym *false*, making (12b) and (12c) paraphrases. This relationship between a sentence and its negation fails in the case of relational antonyms, however:

(13) a   Frieda is George's parent.
      b   Frieda is not George's parent.
      c   George is Frieda's child.

Here, the meaning of (13b) and (13c) are entirely different; hence, a sentence and its negation do not stand in a relationship that's analogous to the relationship between a word and its relational antonym.

Because *parent* and *child* are relational antonyms, if one holds true, the other holds true as well but with a reversal of the subject and object. More interesting is the relationship between negation and gradable antonyms:

(14) a   Harold is tall.
      b   Harold is not tall.
      c   Harold is short.

Although (14b) and (14c) are not strictly speaking paraphrases – Harold could, after all, be of medium height, rendering (14b) true and (14c) false – a person uttering (14b) is typically thought to mean (14c). That is, the meaning of *not X* is often 'strengthened' to an interpretation as the gradable antonym of *X*. One possible reason for this is that if a speaker utters (14b), the hearer has reason to assume Harold's height is relevant and worth mentioning; and if Harold were of average height, that would not be worth mentioning, so Harold must be notably short. (We'll see this sort of explanation grounded in pragmatic theory in the next chapter.) If the context explicitly makes irrelevant the difference between being of average height and being short, the strengthening disappears:

(15) I was hoping the new student would be tall enough to join the basketball team, but Harold is not tall.

Here what's relevant is merely whether or not Harold is tall, not whether he's short or average height, and the suggestion that *not tall* means *short* disappears.

A related phenomenon is what's known in linguistics as 'neg-raising' (because of its effect on syntactic structure). This is exemplified in (16):

(16) I don't like chocolate.

Here the meaning semantically is simply that the speaker has no positive feeling about chocolate – but the intended meaning is typically taken to be that the speaker actually dislikes chocolate. People who 'don't like' chocolate would, semantically speaking, include both those who actively dislike it and those who have no particular opinion one way or the other (hard to imagine, I know). So to 'not like' chocolate covers a wider range of views than to 'dislike' it, which means that reading (16) as meaning that the speaker dislikes chocolate involves a strengthening of what was actually said. Once again, since this is a difference between the semantics and the interpretation, it's an issue of pragmatics.

To get back to our comparison of lexical semantic relations and sentential semantic relations, recall that at the lexical level, homonymy gives rise to ambiguity, so of course including a homonymous form in a sentence can give rise to an ambiguous sentence:

(17) This marker is awfully light.

Here, the ambiguity of the word *light* 'percolates' upward, as it were, to render the entire sentence ambiguous: Is the marker not heavy, or is it not dark? But alongside this sort of ambiguity, which is called **lexical ambiguity**, there's a more interesting type that operates at both the lexical and sentential levels and is based on different structural options. For this reason, it's called **structural ambiguity**, and we've seen cases of it previously. Consider the examples in (18):

(18) a   unbuttonable
     b   unpacked
     c   This sweater is unbuttonable.
     d   My suitcase is unpacked.
     e   I impressed the girl with the dictionary.
     f   I ate the pizza in the fridge.
     g   Greta belongs to an ancient documents reading group.
     h   Time flies like an arrow; fruit flies like a banana.

In (18a), *unbuttonable* can mean either 'able to be unbuttoned' or 'unable to be buttoned', depending on whether you take its structure to be *unbutton+able* or *un+buttonable*. Similarly, *unpacked* in (18b) can be read as either the past tense of *unpack* or 'not packed', which is to say that it can be either *unpack+ed* or *un+packed*. In each case, both options are perfectly acceptable structures that follow the combinatorial rules of English morphology (word structure). And so they give rise to ambiguous sentences with two (or more) perfectly acceptable meanings. In (18c), the sweater in question may or may not have buttons; if it does, those buttons might render it *unbutton+able*, whereas if it doesn't, its lack of buttons might render it *un+buttonable*. In (18d), an *un+packed* suitcase can be a problem if your flight leaves in 30 minutes, whereas an *unpack+ed* suitcase is what you hope to have shortly after you've arrived at your destination.

In (18e), on the other hand, the structural ambiguity isn't based on a single word with more than one possible structural analysis, as in (18a–d), but rather on multiple analyses for the entire sentence. Thus, (18e) can mean either 'I impressed the girl who has the dictionary' or 'I impressed the girl by means of the dictionary', depending on whether or not *the girl with the dictionary* is a single **constituent** or unit within the sentence structure (in this case, a single noun phrase) or whether it's two distinct constituents – the noun phrase *the girl* followed by a separate prepositional phrase *with the dictionary*. A similar ambiguity is seen in (18f), in which one reading has me eating *the pizza in the fridge*, represented by a single noun phrase, whereas the other has me eating the pizza, and doing so in the fridge – a chilly proposition. The *ancient documents reading group* in (18g) is ambiguous in several ways, depending on what gets grouped together as a constituent: Is it a group for reading ancient documents? Is it a reading group for ancient documents? Or is it a documents reading group that has existed for a really long time? It depends entirely on whether you interpret (18g) as *[ancient documents reading] group*, *[ancient documents] [reading group]*, or *ancient [documents reading group]*. Finally, (18h) is a nice example in which both structural and lexical ambiguities combine to render the second clause ambiguous. The humor arises from the fact that the idiom *time flies* leads the reader to give the first clause a structure of *time [flies like an arrow]*, with *flies* having the meaning 'rushes' and *like* the meaning 'similar to' – but then the second clause makes it clear that its intended reading is the less common one, in which the structure is *[fruit flies] [like a banana]*, with *fruit flies* being a type of insect and *like* meaning 'be fond of'. The humor lies in the surprise. (And yes, nothing ruins humor like explaining it.)

Representing meaning

One of the unique problems facing linguists is that the subject of their study – language – is also the medium used to talk about it. Every academic discipline has a set of terms and notations specific to that discipline, and in linguistics this is particularly important. Consider, for example, if you were a field linguist studying a newly discovered language spoken in an area without access to batteries or electricity. You would want to be able to write down how the speakers of this cool new language pronounced their words, but you wouldn't simply want to use English spelling to do so, because English spelling is inconsistent: If the speakers have a word that contains the vowel sound in the English word *be*, should you use an *e*? Or should you spell it *ey*, as in *key*, or *ei*, as in *conceive*, or *ie*, as in *field*, or *ee*, as in *free*, or *y*, as in *happy*, or *ea*, as in *heal*, or *eo*, as in *people*, or . . . And if you decide to go with, say, *e*, that won't solve the problem, because the letter *e* can represent a range of different sounds, as in *be*, *bet*, *women*, *café*, and *erudite*, or can represent no sound at all, as in that final *e* in *erudite*. (And what's up with that *o* in *women* that's pronounced with the same vowel sound as *bin*?) The problem is that just as we've seen that English words can be ambiguous, with one form representing more than one meaning, English spelling can be ambiguous, with one letter representing more than one sound. In the case of sounds, linguists have gotten around the problem by developing the International Phonetic Alphabet, which has a distinct symbol for every sound in human language. Similarly, in the case of meaning, linguists use a system designed to allow them to represent every meaning with a distinct set of symbols. This is a language that's used to describe language – hence, it's a **metalanguage**, a language about language.

It's also, unfortunately, one of the things that strikes fear into the hearts of some linguistics students taking their first semantics class, because the notation can get pretty involved pretty quickly. For our purposes, we'll stick with only the really important symbols, and fortunately there aren't that many of them. Remember that we've been thinking of meaning in terms of truth – and, specifically, in terms of which possible worlds a given proposition is true in. So when we begin to talk about representing meaning, we want to start with a simple way to represent a proposition, and then come up with a way of talking about which possible worlds that proposition is true in.

For cases when it really doesn't matter what the actual meaning of the proposition is, representing it is as simple as it gets: We just use a random letter. By convention, linguists start with the letter p for a single proposition, move to q for a second proposition, and so on up the alphabet as needed. So our proposition p could be 'Alice ate apples' or 'Bill brought Bingo' or 'Carl cuts carrots' or 'Dawn designs doodles' or whatever. Recall that this is what we did at the end of the last chapter, where we were able to talk about the semantics of logical connectives like *and*, *or*, etc. in terms of the effect they had on a set of propositions in worlds where both propositions are true, in worlds where one is true and the other false, etc. And we could represent these effects by means of truth tables.

But our semantic notation wouldn't be very interesting if it couldn't also represent what's inside those individual propositions. So let's look at a little more of the metalanguage linguists have developed for representing semantic meaning. One caveat: There is a LOT more to the metalanguage than what I will present here. But the important thing at this point is just to address the question of **why** such formalisms are useful. If we're merely translating one language (English) into another (our semantic metalanguage), well, that can be (and is!) a lot of fun, but it doesn't get us very far in explaining meaning. So once we've gotten a bit of the semantic metalanguage under our belts, we'll want to see some examples of how it can be useful in showing how linguistic meaning is constructed.

Let's start with the verb. Why? Because in a sense the verb is the heart of the sentence; it drives the structure of the whole thing. If you know your subject is *Edward*, that doesn't tell you much of anything about what the rest of the sentence is going to look like – but if you know your verb is *put*, you suddenly know all kinds of useful things about your sentence structure: You know there's going to be someone (or something) doing the putting, and someone (or something) being put, and a place where that person or thing is being put. In short, you know you'll have a structure like *X put Y Z: Frieda put the fudge in the fridge*, or *Greta put the gravel in the garage*, or *Harold put the haddock on the hamper*. (Okay, I'll stop.) And you know what sorts of things *X*, *Y*, and *Z* will be: *X* will be something that can do something on purpose – we call this an **agent** – and *Y* will be something that can be put somewhere, and *Z* will be some kind of location. And even though the word order can change in interesting ways (more on this in the next chapter!), the respective roles that *X*, *Y*, and *Z* are playing won't change:

(19) a   Harold put the haddock on the hamper.
      b   The haddock was put on the hamper by Harold.
      c   Harold put on the hamper the haddock.

    d   The haddock was put by Harold on the hamper.
    e   On the hamper Harold put the haddock. [. . . On the stairs he put the salmon.]
    f   The haddock Harold put on the hamper. [. . . The tilapia he put on the table.]

Some of these may seem more natural than others, and some are helped along by being uttered in a particular context (for example, when there's a contrast present, as shown in (e) and (f)). But in every case, the three entities in question play the same roles in the sentence, and the verb drives the whole thing, and it's the meaning of this verb that's largely responsible. The act of putting requires someone doing the putting, a thing that's being put, and a place where it's put.

    We'll call the verb a **predicate**. (This, by the way, is a slightly different use of that word from what you may have learned in grade school or high school, where a sentence is sometimes broken down into subjects and predicates.) Our 'notation' for the predicate will just be to put it in all caps:

(20) PUT(harold, haddock, hamper)

And in parentheses after the predicate, as shown in (20), we give its **arguments**, which is to say the participants in the situation being described. The number of arguments a predicate has is its number of **places**. So *sleep* is a one-place predicate, because it doesn't take any kind of object:

(21) a   Myrna slept.
    b   SLEEP(m)
    c   *Myrna slept her dream.

Myrna can sleep, but she can't sleep something. The exception would be a **cognate object**, which would be to use the noun form of the verb as its object: *Myrna slept a deep sleep.* Many verbs that in general don't allow an object will tolerate a cognate object. (Notice also that we're completely ignoring the issue of tense, though a full-blown semantic analysis would of course have to address it.)

The other tiny change I've made in (21) is to just use a lower-case 'm' for Myrna. This is standard practice, and it's easier than writing everything out. But there's also a good reason to do so: Remember that this is a metalanguage, and really, we could use any letter at all as long as we hold its meaning **constant**. If we use a for Myrna, then any a we use is going to be Myrna:

(22) a   Myrna scratched herself.
     b   SCRATCH(a,a)

Showing a certain lack of terminological creativity, we call these letters whose reference remains constant **constants**. In (22), a is a constant. If you want Myrna to scratch Barney, you'd better bring in a second constant:

(23) SCRATCH(a,b)

And so on.

The obvious question to ask at this point is what kind of participant **wouldn't** be constant; presumably Myrna can't change her identity at will. True enough, but sometimes it's handy to be able to vary the participants in a way that we'll see shortly. In that case, we want to use a **variable**. A variable is essentially a place-holder for a participant. Consider (24):

(24) SLEEP(x)

Here we've got a proposition that seems to say 'x sleeps'. But there's a crucial thing to note at this point: This doesn't mean that anyone actually **does** sleep; it's just bringing in the predicate *sleep* and holding a spot for a potential participant. It's what's called an **open proposition**. A complete, or closed, proposition is something that can be true or false. What (24) expresses can't yet be true or false. Open propositions – that is, propositions with one or more unspecified elements – can play a useful role in language. For example, recall that a sentence like (19e) – *On the hamper Harold put the haddock* – becomes more acceptable in a context where it's being contrasted with other things being put in other places; this is to say, it's more acceptable

when the variables in the open proposition in (25) are being filled
with a series of contrasting options:

(25) a   PUT(h,x,y)
    b   A: Where did Harold end up putting all those different fish?
       B: In the fridge he put the flounder, on the hamper he put
       the haddock, on the stairs he put the salmon, on the table he
       put the tilapia. . . .

Similarly, the construction known as a *wh*-cleft requires a certain sort
of open proposition to be salient in the context:

(26) a   What I ate was salmon.
    b   ATE(x,y)

The utterance in (26a) would be extremely odd as my first statement
to my students upon entering a classroom to lecture, because in that
context the open proposition in (26b) – that somebody ate something –
isn't salient. But if a friend is asking me about my dinner in a fancy
restaurant the previous evening, and has asked what everyone in the
group ate, then the open proposition in (26b) is salient and the utterance in (26a) is a perfectly normal thing to say. I'll have more to say in
the next chapter about how an open proposition can make acceptable
the use of certain constructions that otherwise would not be.

    In the meantime, however, if we want to turn an open proposition
into a closed proposition so that we can use it to say something that
can be true or false, we'll need to **bind** the variables. We do this by
using a **quantifier**, which will tell us the quantity of the participants –
starting with either all of the possible participants or one of them.

    Here's what I mean. Setting aside (for now) the fact that we can
have many, few, three, etc. participants, the first and most useful quantifiers are the ones that mean 'all' and 'at least one'. We call these the
universal quantifier (which says the predicate is universally true of
the relevant entities) and the **existential** quantifier (which says there
exists something of which it's true). We use upside-down-and-flipped
versions of capital A (for 'all') and E (for 'exists') to indicate these
quantities, as shown in (27) and (28):

(27) a   Everybody's running.
      b $\forall x(RUN(x))$
(28) a   Somebody's running.
      b $\exists x(RUN(x))$

We read (27b) as 'for all x, x runs' (meaning everything or everybody is running), and we read (28b) as 'there exists an x such that x runs' (meaning there's something or somebody that's running). These are closed propositions because they don't need anything further in order to be able to be either true or false in a given world. To determine whether (27) is true in some world, you look at every entity (every option for what x could be) and see whether it's running. If they all are, then (27) is true. If not, it's false. In (28), you do the same thing, except as soon as you find an entity that's running, you can stop; the proposition is true. One interesting thing to note is that (27) is true even if there's nothing in the world to check. That is, there's no **existential commitment** for the universal; saying that everything is running doesn't mean that anything is running, whereas saying that something is running does, indeed, mean that something is running. This is a great deal clearer if you consider a slightly more complicated proposition:

(29) a   *All philatelists are happy.*
      b $\forall x(P(x){\rightarrow}H(x))$
      c   'for all x, if it's a philatelist, it's happy'
(30) a   *There are happy philatelists.*
      b $\exists x(P(x){\wedge}H(x))$
      c   'there exists an x such that it's a philatelist and it's happy'

(For ease of notation, we've also tightened up our predicate notation to a single letter.) In (29), if there are no philatelists at all, it's still true that anybody who's a philatelist is happy. And this very nicely matches up with that bothersome third row of the truth table for the conditional. But (30) states that there exists at least one entity that is a philatelist who's happy; if there are no philatelists at all, (30) is false.

These examples also show how our quantifiers can interact with our logical connectives. The most common pairing is the combination of a universal with a conditional to mean 'all x's are y', as in (29), and the combination of an existential with a conjunction to mean 'some x's are y', as in (30). Be careful to remember, though, that in this metalanguage there's no semantic difference between *some x's are y* and *there's an x that is y*. *Some* means 'at least one', but not necessarily more than one.

So going back to our possible worlds, if we want to know whether (29) is true in a particular world we no longer have to check every entity in the world; we simply check all the philatelists. This means we have to do two passes: First, we look at each entity to see whether it's a philatelist. Anything that's not a philatelist can be ignored. Now we do a second pass over those philatelists to see whether or not each of them is happy. And not all predicates are verbs; just as things can be either running or not, they can be philatelists or not, and they can be happy or not. A predicate is any property that can be true or false of an entity. So in *Fred is happy*, the predicate is *happy*. In *Fred is a philatelist*, the predicate is *philatelist*.

In each case, the predicate is a **function** operating on some set of objects. That set of objects is the **domain**. And what the function tells us is, for each object in the domain, whether the resulting proposition is true. All of this comes from math, by the way; a function in general operates on the members of a domain to return some value in the **range** (which is just the set of values that are returned). All we really care about is how this works in our metalanguage, which is to say, in our representation of human language. So we'll take a bunch of functions like RUN, HAPPY, and PHILATELIST, and apply each of them to, say, Guinevere and see whether the resulting proposition is true or not in a given world:

(31) a R(g)
      b H(g)
      c P(g)

Now, whether Guinevere is actually running, or happy, or a philatelist, in the actual world or any other, is unknown to me, so I can't tell you whether each function will return the value 'true' or 'false'. But we can apply them to someone I do know about, which is me, Betty:

(32) a R(b) = f
      b H(b) = t
      c P(b) = f

Which is to say, I'm not running (actually, I'm typing), and I'm not a philatelist, but I am happy. Now, back to our happy and unhappy philatelists in (29), repeated here as (33):

(33) a *All philatelists are happy.*
b $\forall x(P(x) \to H(x))$
c 'for all *x*, if it's a philatelist, it's happy'

Here, both P and H are functions applying consecutively to every possible value of *x* in the domain (that is, every entity in a particular possible world). First we find all the entities for which P(x) is true (that is, all the philatelists), and then we check whether, for each of those entities, H(x) is true (that is, whether they're happy). If for every value of *x*, P(x)$\to$H(x), which is to say that if it's in the set of philatelists it's also in the set of happy things, then the whole complex proposition *All philatelists are happy* is true. Now, this may strike you as pretty obvious, but remember that we're trying to get at the meaning of *All philatelists are happy*, so it's actually a good thing if the result strikes a native speaker of English as being obviously correct.

Okay, so now we have a handy metalinguistic notation that corresponds to the sentence *All philatelists are happy.* What does this gain us? The answer is that not only have we escaped the ambiguities of natural language; we now in fact have a way of representing those ambiguities. And if our metalanguage can actually represent each meaning of an ambiguous sentence differently, it means that we've come much closer to having a one-to-one representation between our notation and our possible set of meanings – and, in turn, that we've found a useful way of representing meaning. And if we've got a useful, unambiguous way of representing meaning, we've got a useful, unambiguous way of talking about meaning.

So let's take a moment to look at some cases of ambiguity in natural language and how our semantic metalanguage deals with them. First, there's the common problem encountered in restaurant menus, where you see a set of options like the one in (34):

(34) With an entrée, customers may have soup and side salad or salad bar.

There are two possible readings of this. One reading is that either you can have soup and a side salad, or alternatively you can have the salad bar. The other reading is that you get soup either way, but you have a choice between a side salad and the salad bar. The two possibilities for what customers may have are informally represented in (35):

(35) a   (soup∧side-salad)∨salad bar
     b   soup∧(side-salad∨salad bar)

That is, in (35a) a customer may have either the pair 'soup and side salad' or the salad bar, whereas in (35b) they may have soup and either the side salad or the salad bar.

Another example of ambiguity in natural language that is disambiguated in our metalanguage is what's called **scope ambiguity**. This notion of **scope** is similar to its lay definition: the extent to which something applies (as in the scope of a project). So when a quantifier has scope over a variable, it applies to that variable:

(36) $\forall x(R(x))$

Here, the universal quantifier has scope over the variable inside of $R(x)$. If it didn't, that variable would be unbound (or **free**), and we'd once again be stuck with an open proposition. Consider, for example, (37):

(37) $\forall x(R(x))\wedge(J(x))$

Assume R stands for 'runs' and J stands for 'jumps'. Initially it looks like (37) says that for all x, x runs and jumps – hence that everything runs and jumps – but if you look more closely, you'll see that the set of parentheses that opens right after $\forall x$ closes right after $R(x)$. And for that reason, that's where the scope of the universal quantifier ends; it doesn't have scope over $J(x)$, and therefore it doesn't bind that last x. Which in turn means that what (37) says is: Everything runs, and x jumps. We don't know whether anything at all jumps, or everything jumps, or some things jump, or . . . well, we don't know anything about what does or doesn't jump until that variable is bound by a quantifier.

Now, here's where it gets interesting. If we line up a couple of quantifiers, the outer one has scope over the inner one. So for example, consider (38):

(38) a $\forall x \exists y (BOOK(y) \wedge LIKE(x,y))$
     b $\exists y \forall x (BOOK(y) \wedge LIKE(x,y))$

The first thing to notice is that these two formulas are identical except for the ordering of $\forall x$ and $\exists y$ at the beginning. We say that in (38a) $\forall x$ has **wide scope** and $\exists y$ has **narrow scope**, whereas in (38b) $\exists y$ has wide scope and $\forall x$ has narrow scope. What's interesting is that this difference corresponds to a difference in meaning: (38a) informally reads 'for all x there exists a y such that y is a book and x likes y' – or 'for every individual, there exists a book they like'. In (38b), on the other hand, an informal reading would be 'there exists a y such that for all x, y is a book and x likes y' – or 'there exists a book that everyone likes'. (Technically we'd also want our formula to state that x is a person, but I'm glossing over that for clarity.)

So here's how the meanings line up:

(39) a $\forall x \exists y (BOOK(y) \wedge LIKE(x,y))$ 'Everyone likes a book'
     b $\exists y \forall x (BOOK(y) \wedge LIKE(x,y))$ 'There's a book everyone likes'

The crucial difference is that in (39a) the book might differ from person to person, but in (39b) the existential has wide scope and so there exists a single book for which the rest of the proposition holds – a single book that everyone likes.

A **scope ambiguity** is an ambiguity in natural language in which the two different meanings correspond to two different scopes, as in (40):

(40) a   Everyone loves someone.
     b   Someone loves everyone.

Each of these sentences is ambiguous. In (40a), the most natural reading is that each person loves some other person (with a potentially different loved one for each person), but there's also a reading in which there's one individual whom everyone loves. These two readings correspond to the following formulas:

(41) a $\forall x \exists y (L(x,y))$ 'Each person loves another person'
     b $\exists y \forall x (L(x,y))$ 'There's a person everyone loves'

In (41a), the meaning is 'for all x, there's a y such that x loves y', whereas in (41b), it's 'there exists a y such that for all x, x loves y'. Again, the difference boils down to whether there's one person being loved or a (potentially) different loved one for each person, and this difference depends on whether the existential has narrow scope (41a) or wide scope (41b).

In (40b), *Someone loves everyone*, the two possibilities are 'there's a person who loves everyone' and the somewhat less natural reading 'everyone is loved by another person'. Notice that these are distinct from the two meanings in (41). Here are the formulas for these readings:

(42) a $\exists x \forall y (L(x,y))$ 'There's a person who loves everyone'
      b $\forall y \exists x (L(x,y))$ 'Everyone is loved by another person'

If you compare the formulas in (41) with those in (42), you'll see that they exhaust the possible orderings of the universal quantifier, the existential quantifier, and the two variables x and y. And each possible ordering corresponds to a distinct meaning. It would seem that this metalanguage does indeed move us toward our goal of having a one-to-one correspondence between form and meaning – an unambiguous way of representing the meanings we express in human language. We haven't fully attained that goal, because there's a huge range of meanings we can express in human language, most of which are far more complex than what we've had space to deal with here. But hopefully the discussion so far has given you a sense of why we'd want to go to the trouble of developing a semantic metalanguage, and what such a language can do for us in our effort to understand meaning in natural language.

Building complex meanings out of simple meanings

I've made a point of noting the commonalities between lexical semantics and sentential semantics largely because it helps us to see how the meanings of words contribute to the meaning of the sentences containing them. Recall that we said the meanings of certain words (like intransitive verbs and adjectives) are what it takes for the word to be true of something – that is, the meaning of *run* is what it takes for something to be truthfully said to be running. And the **denotation** of the word *run* is everything for which it can truthfully be said that it runs – that is, the set of running things. On the flip side, by looking at the set of running things, one ought to be able to reliably pick out what it is that they have in common, i.e., what property is characteristic of that set of things.

Recall also that *run* corresponds to a function – call it RUN – that applies to a set of things in a given world and returns either the value 'true' or the value 'false'. So the denotation of *run* is the set of entities for which the function RUN returns the value 'true'. And that, in turn, is just a slightly fancier way of saying what we said at the outset, that the meaning of *run* is what it takes for something to be truthfully said to be running – i.e., for something to be in the denotation of *run*.

Since the denotation of *run* is the set of things that share one particular characteristic (which is the fact that they're running), and that characteristic is what causes the value 'true' to be returned when the function RUN is applied to the members of that denotation, we say that RUN is the **characteristic function** of that set. Again, this just means that the set of entities that constitute the denotation of *run* – the set of running things – are characterized by the function RUN. They are the set of all and only the entities for which RUN(x) is true.

On the one hand, this results in the eye-rollingly obvious notion that the meaning of *run* is whatever it is that all running things share. On the other hand, it ties everything we've said about the meanings of words together with everything we've said about the meanings of sentences. And, more importantly, it gives us a glimmer of how meaning can be **compositional** – that is, how it can be the case that larger, sentence-sized meanings are built up out of smaller, word-sized meanings. If our theory of word meaning and our theory of sentence meaning were unrelated, we would never be able to build up word meanings in such a way as to derive sentence meanings, and a compositional semantics would remain beyond our reach.

Compositionality also requires that we be able to show what sorts of rules we implicitly follow in building up sentences out of words, and hence in building sentence meanings out of word meanings. This requires us to take at least a quick look at **syntax**, which is the structure of sentences and how individual words combine to create phrases, which in turn combine to create sentences. For a truly compositional semantics, we'll need to be able to correlate the build-up of word meanings into sentence meanings with the build-up of words into sentences, which is to say that we'll need to be able to correlate semantics with syntax. Since this isn't a syntax textbook – and because syntax itself can get crazy complicated – I won't delve too deeply into the details, but it will be enlightening to get at least a sense of how syntax and semantics can be built up in parallel.

Just as semantics is the study of what a speaker of a language knows about expressing meaning in that language, syntax is the study of what a speaker of a language knows about acceptable sentence structures in that language. To know the syntax of English is to know what is and isn't an acceptable ordering of the words in English – to know that (43a) is fine but (43b) isn't:

(43) a   I need to buy a bag to keep my snacks in.
      b   *Bag to buy a snacks my keep to in I need.

And if you've had it drilled into your head your whole life that a sentence mustn't end with a preposition, you may be squirming a bit, worrying that (43a) isn't actually fine. But remember that as linguists, we take a **descriptive**, not a **prescriptive**, approach to language. Descriptively, (43a) is indeed fine, because people overwhelmingly would choose that phrasing over something hideous like *I need to buy a bag in which to keep my snacks.* Regardless of what a few overly stuffy grammarians might say, (43a) is a grammatical sentence of English – and to see the difference between that and a truly ungrammatical sentence, look no further than (43b), which no speaker of English would ever produce (and few speakers of English would be able to comprehend even if it were produced).

A complete syntax of English would ideally be a way to determine what is and isn't a sentence of English. Just listing all the sentences won't work; there are too many of them (an infinite number, as we'll see shortly). So we'll need a set of rules to determine what is and isn't okay in terms of word order. Instead of making lists of actual sentences, our rules can refer to entire classes of words, such as nouns, verbs, etc. – that is, the **parts of speech**. But if we have a separate rule for every possible ordering of these parts of speech, it will again quickly become unmanageable. For example, we'd need a dizzying array of rules just to allow for the relatively straightforward sentences in (44):

(44) a   Sammy sneezed.
    b   Sammy devoured the fish.
    c   Sammy gave the fish some food.
    d   Sammy put the fish into a bowl.
    e   Sammy put the fish on the edge of the table.
    f   A member of the family put the fish on the edge of the table.

Here we see that a sentence can be made up of a noun plus a verb, or a noun plus a verb plus a determiner (*the*) plus a noun, or a noun plus a verb plus a determiner plus a noun plus another determiner plus another noun . . . and that's obviously unhelpful. It's much easier if we combine, for example, the 'optional-determiner plus noun' combo into a **noun phrase**, which allows us to come up with a more reasonable set of rules for sentence structure (where 'S' means 'sentence', 'NP' means 'noun phrase', 'P' means 'preposition', and an arrow means 'can be made up of'). Doing that, we get the following rules to account for our sentences in (44):

(45) a   S → NP V
    b   S → NP V NP
    c   S → NP V NP NP
    d   S → NP V NP P NP
    e   S → NP V NP P NP P NP
    f   S → NP P NP V NP P NP P NP

But you can see that this way of listing the allowable structures of English would still quickly get out of control. More importantly, this list of possibilities obviously can't be what children acquire when they acquire English. For one thing, there's no upper bound on the length of a grammatical English sentence:

(46) Sammy put the fish into the bowl on top of the refrigerator in the kitchen of the house down the block around the corner in the town over the hill beyond the meadows in the countryside in the

portion of the nation alongside an ocean of fish with a mass of seaweed along the edge of the tectonic plate below the. . . .

Well, you get the picture. What this tells us is that the rules for creating a sentence can't end up being just a string listing the contents of the sentence; the set of rules needs to have enough structure to generate an infinite number of sentences by means of a finite (in fact, quite short) list of rules.

We could of course tighten things up significantly by taking the preposition+NP combo (e.g., *in the kitchen*) to be a prepositional phrase (PP); then the rules in (45) boil down to:

(47) a   S → NP V
    b   S → NP V NP
    c   S → NP V NP NP
    d   S → NP V NP PP
    e   S → NP V NP PP PP
    f   S → NP PP V NP PP PP

But again, ultimately this won't fix the problem of an infinite number of sentences. What does fix it is recognizing that the combination of an NP and a PP can itself be an NP. We know this because *the cookies* and *the cookies on the table* can appear in all the same places in a sentence:

(48) a   The cookies are warm.
    b   The cookies on the table are warm.
    c   John gave the cookies to Fred.
    d   John gave the cookies on the table to Fred.
    e   Fred told Celia about the cookies.
    f   Fred told Celia about the cookies on the table.

We can capture this fact in our rules by writing a rule for the structure of an NP that allows it to contain an optional PP.

Similarly, a verb alone (V) and a verb plus a noun phrase (V NP) behave alike:

(49) a   Amy ran.
    b   Amy ran the meeting.

c What Amy wants to do is run.

 d What Amy wants to do is run the meeting.

We'll consider each of these options to constitute a verb phrase (VP), which means we'll want a rule for the structure of a VP that allows it to contain an optional NP. So instead of the set of rules in (47), we can substitute those in (50), where 'D' stands for 'determiner' and optional elements are indicated by parentheses:

(50) a S → NP VP

  b NP → (D) N (PP)

  c PP → P (NP)

  d VP → V (NP)

These rules tell us that a sentence is made up of an NP and a VP, an NP is made up of a required noun optionally preceded by a determiner and/ or followed by a PP, a PP is made up of a required P plus an optional NP, and a VP is made up of a required V plus an optional NP. We say that the required noun is the **head** of a noun phrase, the required preposition is the head of a prepositional phrase, and the required verb is the head of a verb phrase. The optional phrase to the right of the head in these rules is called a **complement**. (There is actually an important distinction between two types of embedded phrases – complements and adjuncts – that we will ignore as irrelevant for our purposes.)

 The great thing about the rules in (50) is that we don't need to keep adding new rules to accommodate longer and longer sentences such as we find in (44) and (46). Instead, we've built a wonderful little circularity into these four rules: An NP can contain a PP, which in turn can contain an NP, which in turn can contain a PP, which in turn can contain an NP, which in turn can contain a PP, and on indefinitely. This circularity is called **recursion**, and it makes it possible for a small number of rules to generate an infinite number of sentences. And indeed these four rules are all that are needed to account for (46), in which everything from *into the bowl* onward is one massive PP, made up of a P (*into*) plus an NP, which turn is made up of *the bowl* plus another PP, which contains another NP, which contains another PP. . . . This results in a structure for the sentence that isn't linear – just one long strung-together mess of words and phrases – but rather is **hierarchical**, with phrases inside of phrases inside of phrases.

At this point, you can probably begin to see how it's possible for a child to acquire a language effortlessly: The child doesn't have to learn an infinite list of possible strings, but rather a quite small list of ordering principles for the language in question. For example, a child acquiring English needn't learn the rules in (50b), (50c), and (50d) individually; instead, they'll see that inside of an English phrase, the head consistently precedes its optional complement, and this tells them everything they would have learned from memorizing a whole bunch of rules like those in (50b), (50c), and (50d). (Except for the bit about the determiner, which in a more fully fleshed-out syntax is actually handled elsewhere.) In short, this gives us a brief taste of how a very long and complex set of sentences can be generated by an extremely simple syntax.

Similarly, when we say a transitive verb requires an object NP, it doesn't matter at all how simple or complex that NP is:

(51) a   Sammy devoured fish.
     b   Sammy devoured the fish from the bowl on top of the refrigerator in the kitchen of the house down the block around the corner in the town over the hill beyond the meadows in the countryside in the portion of the nation alongside an ocean of fish with a mass of seaweed along the edge of the tectonic plate below. . . .

Each of these is an instantiation of the rule 'VP → V NP'; that is, in each of them the verb is followed by a single noun phrase.

But this simple set of rules now presents a further problem: It lets us generate all kinds of ungrammatical sentences, such as those in (52):

(52) a   *Gloria devoured.
     b   *Herman sneezed the book.
     c   *Irene put the bottle.

If we have a rule that says a VP can be made up of just a verb, why isn't (52a) acceptable? And if our rules say that a VP can be made up of a verb plus an NP, why aren't (52b) and (52c) acceptable? Once again, if we want to capture the ungrammaticality of the sentences in (52) through purely structural rules, we'll need rules of unimaginable complexity. But there's another option, which is to derive these structures from other parts of the grammar.

Recall that we said the verb is the heart of the sentence, and to a great degree determines what the structure of the sentence will be. The simplest example is the difference between a **transitive** verb, which takes a direct object, and an **intransitive** verb, which does not:

(53) a   Sammy devoured the fish.
   b   Sammy sneezed.

Knowing that the subject of a sentence is *Sammy* doesn't tell us much about what the rest of the sentence will look like, but knowing that the verb is *devoured* does: It tells us that there will be both a subject and an object. It also tells us something about the semantics of those two participants: If we know that the verb is *devour*, we also know that the subject is the sort of thing that can devour things, and that the object will be the sort of thing that can be devoured. That is – unless we're speaking metaphorically (as in *The tsunami devoured the city*) – we can expect the subject to be an animate **agent** and the object to be an edible **theme**. An agent is an entity that is acting intentionally (few of us devour things accidentally), and the theme is what's being affected or acted upon. The subject, object, and indirect object are called **arguments** of a verb. A **one-place** verb takes a single argument, which is why trying to give a one-place verb like *sneeze* a second argument, as in (52b), is ungrammatical. Similarly, a **two-place** verb takes two arguments, which is why using a two-place verb like *devour* with only one argument, as in (52a), is also ungrammatical.

This phenomenon is called **subcategorization**, which is just to say that the category of verbs can be broken down further into subcategories based on how many arguments the verb takes. And this subcategorization doesn't only care about NP arguments; verbs may also take other types of arguments:

(54) a   Linda put the figurine on the mantle.
   b   *Linda put the figurine.
   c   Marilyn went to the store.

    d   *Marilyn went.
    e   Norbert felt funny.
    f   *Norbert felt.

In (54a) and (54b), we see that *put* subcategorizes for both an NP and a PP (as well as, of course, a subject, which usually isn't mentioned because it's always required in English). In (54c) and (54d), we see that *went* subcategorizes for a PP. And in (54e) and (54f), we see that *felt* subcategorizes for an adjective phrase. (Here it's a single word, but it could have been a longer phrase, such as *very funny* or *quite surprisingly funny*.)

The crucial thing to note is that part of what it means to know a verb is to know its **subcategorization frame** – the set of arguments it takes. And this isn't always completely predictable from its meaning. For example, the words *hide* and *conceal* are similar in meaning:

(55) a   Oliver hid the herring.
       b   Oliver concealed the cod.

But they differ in terms of their subcategorization:

(56) a   Oliver hid.
       b   *Oliver concealed.

It's fine for Oliver to hide, but it's not okay for Oliver to conceal. Notice that this isn't simply a difference in meaning, since both meanings would presumably be the same as those in (57):

(57) a   Oliver hid himself.
       b   Oliver concealed himself.

So it's not the case that (56b) is bad because there's something objectionable about what it would mean; rather, it's an arbitrary fact about the argument-taking properties of the verb *conceal*. To learn the verb *conceal* is to learn its pronunciation, its meaning, its part of speech (verb), and the fact that it takes two arguments. To learn the verb *hide* is to learn its pronunciation, its meaning, its part of speech, and the fact that it may take either a single argument or two arguments.

The set of syntactic rules, then, can include optional elements, because part of what it means to know a verb is to know which of these elements are required, optional, or disallowed. Since the speaker's knowledge of a verb will tell them what the syntax of the sentence will look like, this doesn't have to be specified in our phrase structure rules. And this in turn means that a child acquiring English can acquire only a very minimal number of rules (like the one that says that the head of phrase in English comes before its complement), and this knowledge will combine with their knowledge of a verb's argument-taking properties to tell them a vast amount about what does and doesn't count as an acceptable English sentence. Indeed, those two pieces of information alone will generate an infinite number of acceptable English sentence structures.

As I mentioned above, not only does knowing a verb include knowing how many arguments it takes, but it also includes knowing the roles those arguments will play – for example, whether the subject is constrained to be a purposefully acting **agent** or a non-agentive **theme**, i.e., the person or thing affected. We call this an argument's **thematic role**. Consider the sentences in (58):

(58) a   Priscilla jumped over the puddle.
     b   The ice melted.
     c   Priscilla melted the ice with a blowtorch.
     d   Priscilla rolled down the hill.

In (58a), *Priscilla* counts as an agent because she is purposely jumping. In (58b), *the ice* isn't an agent, because it's not melting on purpose; the melting is just something that's happening to it. In this case it's considered a theme. In (58c), *Priscilla* is again the agent, and *the ice* is again the theme. What this shows is that an argument's thematic role is distinct from its syntactic role: *The ice* is a syntactic subject in (58b) and an object in (58c), but its thematic role is the same. And finally, in (58d), the sentence is ambiguous between a reading in which Priscilla rolled down the hill purposely and a reading in which her rolling down the hill is the result of some other cause, as in (59):

(59) a   Priscilla lay down in the soft grass and rolled down the hill for the pure joy of it.

b   Running down the steep slope, Priscilla tripped on a stone, fell, and rolled halfway down the hill before she could stop herself.

In (59a) *Priscilla* is an agent, whereas in (59b) she is a theme. The ambiguity in (58d) reflects these two thematic roles; hence, (58d) could describe either scenario.

We saw above with *hide* and *conceal* that verbs with similar meanings may be subject to different syntactic argument-taking properties; *hide* can take either a single argument or two arguments, whereas *conceal* must take (at least) two arguments. And we've just seen that a verb's arguments may play the same thematic role in different syntactic positions, or multiple thematic roles in a single syntactic position. So while it remains true that the verb determines both the subcategorization frame (i.e., how many arguments, and of what type, it requires) and the thematic roles of the arguments (agent, theme, and many others), there is no fixed relationship between the semantics of a verb and the syntax of the sentence it appears in. It might be more accurate to say that the meaning of a verb constrains the options available for the structure of a sentence; within those constraints, the speaker has a range of options for how to arrange the arguments within the sentence. Different verbs allow different sets of options, in a way that is partly but not completely determined by their meanings. Consider, for example, the sentences in (60)–(62):

(60) a   Priscilla melted the ice with a blowtorch.
      b   The blowtorch melted the ice.
      c   The ice melted.
(61) a   Steve opened the door with a key.
      b   The key opened the door.
      c   The door opened.
(62) a   Theresa shattered the vase with a hammer.
      b   The hammer shattered the vase.
      c   The vase shattered.

In each case, the verb allows a three-argument option, with agent, theme, and **instrument** (the means by which the action is carried out), as well as a two-argument option with instrument and theme, and a one-argument option with only the theme. What's interesting is that for all of the many verbs that participate in this alternation, the positioning of the arguments in the syntactic frame for each variant remains the same; if only one argument appears, for instance, it will be the theme, and it will appear in subject position. (And note that if two arguments appear, either the instrument or the agent can be the subject; i.e., you also get *Priscilla melted the ice,* etc.)

This set of patterns is one of many such patterns in English that specific sets of verbs engage in, known as **verb alternations**. There are many verbs that don't participate in the alternation, such as *kick*:

(63) a Vera kicked the ball with her foot.
　　 b Her foot kicked the ball.
　　 c #The ball kicked.

Another example is what's called the **middle** alternation. You're probably familiar with the difference between active and passive voice, but English also has a less commonly used middle voice:

(64) a The man sliced the bread.
　　 b The bread was sliced by the man.
　　 c The bread sliced easily.
(65) a Wade embarrassed Zelda.
　　 b Zelda was embarrassed by Wade.
　　 c Zelda embarrasses easily.
(66) a Ariel answered the phone.
　　 b The phone was answered by Ariel.
　　 c ?#The phone answered easily.

In each of the above examples, the (a) variant illustrates the active voice, the (b) variant illustrates the passive voice, and the (c) variant illustrates the middle voice. As you can see, the verbs *slice* and *embarrass* allow the middle voice, but the verb *answer* does not. As a final example, consider (67)–(69):

(67) a Bella loaded bananas onto the boat.
　　 b Bella loaded the boat with bananas.
(68) a Carl spread butter onto the bread.

   b   Carl spread the bread with butter.
(69) a   Diego sprayed paint onto the wall.
   b   Diego sprayed the wall with paint.

Not only does this class of verbs allow the alternation seen in these examples, but it also adds a neat secondary effect: In each of the (b) examples, there is a sense of completeness that is lacking in (a). That is, if Bella loaded a half-dozen bananas onto the boat, it's reasonable to describe that scenario using (67a), but it's not reasonable to describe it with (67b); Bella has loaded the boat with bananas only if she has loaded it to capacity or at least somewhere near capacity. Likewise, *Carl spread butter onto the bread* seems like a reasonable way to describe Carl spreading a bit of butter onto the corner of a piece of bread, but *Carl spread the bread with butter* doesn't. And likewise in (69), where (69a) seems like a more appropriate way to describe Diego's spraying a bit of paint onto a corner of the wall than (69b) does.

   There are many, many more such alternations, described in detail in Levin (1993). This is a fruitful area for research, because it stands at the interface between syntax and semantics, and there remains a great deal still to learn about how these two aspects of our linguistic knowledge interact and affect each other. In the next chapter we'll look at some additional options that language gives us for varying the order of words in a sentence.

Opaque contexts: filtering meaning through belief

We've seen how semanticists and philosophers of language rely on the notion of truth for their theories of meaning, and we've also seen how the notion of compositionality suggests that smaller units (like words) can be built up in a predictable way into larger units (like phrases, simple sentences, and complex sentences). This in turn suggests that the meanings of larger units will be predictable from those of smaller units and the rules for combining them. But it doesn't mean that the truth or falsity of a smaller unit will automatically 'percolate up' to a larger unit that contains it. Recall the issue of propositional-attitude verbs from Chapter 2, where we found that (70a) below can be true while (70b) is false, despite the fact that chickpeas and garbanzo beans are the same thing:

(70) a Celia believes that garbanzo beans are round.
      b Celia believes that chickpeas are round.

Because *believe* is a verb that describes Celia's attitude toward the proposition in question, what matters for the truth-value of the complex sentence is simply whether or not she holds the stated belief; whether that belief is true or not is irrelevant to the sentence as a whole. And since Celia may be wrong about what a garbanzo bean is, what a chickpea is, and/or the fact that they are identical, she can hold any belief at all about their shape, and does not have to believe that a chickpea's shape is the same as that of a garbanzo bean. The truth of the sentence in (70a) does not depend directly on whether garbanzo beans are in fact round, but only on whether or not Celia believes that they are; the truth of the embedded sentence is not preserved in the compositional process of building up from smaller units of meaning into a larger unit of meaning. Because this is a reliable result of the use of a certain class of verbs, which in turn are identifiable by their meaning, it is not a particularly worrisome threat to compositionality. Just as we know what the effect of a logical operator will be on the meaning of the propositions on which it operates, we know what the effect of a propositional-attitude verb will be on the proposition that constitutes its complement.

We say that the position following a propositional-attitude verb is an **opaque context**; the truth of the embedded proposition cannot "shine through" to the complex proposition. The truth-value of the sentence as a whole does not survive replacing, say, *garbanzo beans* in the embedded sentence with *chickpeas*, even though we would normally expect the replacing of one noun phrase with a co-referential noun phrase to preserve truth. But again, since the meaning of the sentence as a whole has to do with an individual's beliefs about the embedded sentence's truth and not its actual truth, we can breathe a sigh of relief, knowing that this is not a threat to a compositional approach to semantics.

We've taken a view of sentential meaning that is based on the states of affairs a sentence can truthfully be applied to, which is to say the set of worlds it picks out from among all possible worlds. But there's more to meaning than truth; we can use a semantically true (or false) sentence to convey a wide range of meanings that transcend notions of truth and falsity, and what we intend to convey will differ from context to context. Moreover, part of the context is our set of beliefs, and our set of beliefs about each others' beliefs. We've seen that opaque contexts are one situation in which the sentential context in which a proposition is embedded will affect the truth-value of that proposition, but there's a lot more to the context of an utterance than its sentential context; there's also the context of who said it, and where, and why, and so forth. The question, then, is to what extent there exists a consistent set of rules or principles we follow in building up from semantic meaning to meaning-in-context. And that is a job for pragmatics.

Chapter 4

Pragmatics

Thus far we have taken a truth-conditional, compositional approach to semantic meaning, in which the semantic meaning of a chunk of language is related in a predictable way to its truth in a given world and in which larger meanings are related in a predictable way to the smaller meanings of which they are composed. But surely what it means to 'mean' something involves the speaker's intent in saying it, not just its truth-conditions. Indeed, this is one of the primary senses of the word *mean*: When I say that *I didn't mean you couldn't go to the party*, I'm not necessarily objecting to the truth-conditions of what I've previously said; rather, I'm objecting to a possible interpretation of my intention. And when we're talking about interpretations and intentions, we've moved beyond the realm of semantics. Now we've entered the realm of pragmatics.

Implicature: what you say vs. what you mean

You may recall that the truth tables in Chapter 2 made you feel a little uneasy, as though they didn't really capture what a word like *and* or *if* actually means when it's used by real people in a real context. For example, in the following three examples, the word *and* seems to have three different meanings:

(1) a   I need to clean the house and I need to walk the dog.
    b   Form the dough into a ball and allow it to rise for two hours.
    c   Adele landed an important client and was given a sizeable bonus.

In (1a), there is no ordering or causative relationship between clean-ing the house and walking the dog; they are merely two things I need to do. This meaning is the one most closely reflected by the truth table for conjunction. In (1b), there is a strong sense that the word *and* imposes an ordering: You might grudgingly acknowledge that if you first allow the dough to rise and then form it into a ball you'll have technically obeyed the instructions, but you know perfectly well that your attempt to make bread will be a failure; it's clear to any speaker of English that the intention behind (1b) is that you first form the dough into a ball and then allow it to rise for two hours. But there's still no sense of causation: You're not allowing it to rise because you formed it into a ball; you're allowing it to rise because otherwise the bread will be too dense. In (1c), however, you get a sense that the first clause is the cause of the second, i.e., that the word *and* means not just that both conjuncts are true, but also that the events occurred in that order, and moreover that Adele's bonus was a direct result of her landing an important client. Thus, the meaning of *and* in (1b) and (1c) seems to go beyond what we saw in the truth table. Similar discrep-ancies between the truth tables and natural-language meanings arise for the other connectives.

Faced with these discrepancies, there are a couple of ways we could react. One way would be to decide that, for example, *and* is three-ways ambiguous among the meanings illustrated in (1) above (and similarly for the other connectives). A second approach would be to try to see whether we can rescue the logical meanings of the connectives by establishing a consistent relationship between their logical senses and their use in human language. This is the approach taken by philoso-pher H.P. Grice in his seminal paper "Logic and Conversation" (Grice 1975). He set out to show that the logical meanings of the connectives are in fact their semantic meanings, and that the additional meanings they take on when used in actual human discourse are due to an inter-action between these semantic meanings and a separate principle that interlocutors follow and on the basis of which they draw conclusions about each other's meaning. This paper not only saved the word *and* from being (at least) three-ways ambiguous, but also became the foun-dation of a vast amount of work in pragmatics – the study of language use in context. In short, it provides a road map to get us from what a speaker has semantically **said** to what they have pragmatically **meant**.

Grice (1957) first distinguished between **natural** and **non-natural** meaning. Recall from Chapter 1 that natural meaning is a direct relationship between a stimulus and what it indicates, as with *Those clouds mean rain.* It's not intentional, and it's not arbitrary; clouds don't intend to mean rain, and they couldn't decide to mean something else. Non-natural meaning, on the other hand, is intentional and arbitrary. We as a society have decided that a red octagon means 'stop'. We decided it intentionally, and the choice was more or less arbitrary, in the sense that we could just as well have decided that a blue circle means 'stop'. Human language is an instance of non-natural meaning: We use it with the intention of conveying specific meanings, and with very minor exceptions (such as **onomatopoeic** words like *woof*), the relationship between a meaning and the word that conveys it is arbitrary. This latter point is made clear by the mere fact of there being roughly 7,000 languages in the world: If the word *table* weren't simply an arbitrary label for the thing it designates, it wouldn't be the case that other languages have altogether different arbitrary labels for the same thing. A table could just as well have ended up being called a *dog* in English; the fact that it's called a *table* is an accident of linguistic history. Nonetheless, on any given occasion of its use, the speaker intends it to mean what we've all agreed the word *table* should mean. On the other hand, if we're at dinner and I ask *Is there any salt on the table?*, you're likely to recognize this as an indirect request for salt; and this is a meaning that goes well beyond the literal meaning of the question, just as causation goes well beyond the literal meaning of the word *and.*

Thus, human language has an aspect of convention (what we've all more or less arbitrarily agreed a word or sentence means, regardless of context) and an aspect of intention (what I as a speaker want to convey by using it in the current context). Roughly speaking, the conventional meaning is covered by semantics, and the intentional meaning is covered by pragmatics. So the question at hand for Grice was: How do we get from the conventional meaning to the intentional meaning?

His answer is brilliant in its simplicity: We assume that we're both trying to be cooperative, and we interpret each other's utterances accordingly. Grice (1975) sets forth the **Cooperative Principle**, which in effect says 'be cooperative'. As he actually phrased it, the CP is somewhat more wordy:

The Cooperative Principle

Make your conversational contribution such as is required, at the stage at which it occurs, by the accepted purpose or direction of the talk exchange in which you are engaged.

(Grice 1975:45)

This, of course, boils down to 'say what's appropriate, given the current stage and purpose of the conversation' – or simply 'say what's appropriate' – or even more simply 'be cooperative'. Notice that even when we might think we're being uncooperative – when we're arguing, for example – we're still being cooperative in terms of our conversational contribution: We say things that are appropriate at the current stage of the argument, we say things that we believe to be true, we say things that are relevant, we say things in a reasonable order, etc. If we weren't going to try to cooperate in this very basic sense, there would hardly be any point in speaking at all.

From Grice's point of view, for a speaker to say too much or too little, or to say what they know to be false or irrelevant, is simply uncooperative. Since we presumably want our hearer to be able to figure out our meaning, it's to our advantage to be cooperative – and in the case of communication, being cooperative means making our meaning recognizable. The hearer's job, then, is to try to determine how the speaker's utterance can count as cooperative. If what the speaker has said seems to be in some way irrelevant, disordered, obviously untrue, etc., the hearer will go to great lengths to come up with a way in which it is still cooperative in the sense of having a meaning that can reasonably be figured out given the context, the utterance itself, and the speaker's and hearer's beliefs about each other. In this sense, all of communication is a cooperative venture between a speaker and a hearer working together to make meaning.

To flesh this out, Grice developed certain **maxims** of the CP. These maxims are phrased like commands – "be relevant," for example – but aren't actually prescriptive in nature. After all, nobody has to tell speakers to be relevant; we do it automatically, and if we didn't, our hearers wouldn't be able to follow our line of thought. Instead, the maxims are descriptive, describing how interlocutors actually behave in conversation. For the sake of accuracy, I should note that Grice himself listed four categories under which he placed the maxims; these categories he labeled **Quantity**, **Quality**, **Relation**, and **Manner**. Within each category are maxims relating to that category. Overwhelmingly, however, usage among linguists has been to call these the four maxims of the CP – the maxim of Quantity, the maxim of Quality, the maxim of Relation, and the maxim of Manner – and to make reference then to sub-maxims of these maxims. Having pointed out the slight inaccuracy in current usage, I'll go ahead and follow it, since Grice himself would probably consider an obstinate and obfuscatory adherence to his original wording to be unnecessarily unclear and, hence, uncooperative.

The maxims of the Cooperative Principle, then, are these (Grice 1975:45–46):

Quantity

1   Make your contribution as informative as is required (for the current purposes of the exchange).
2   Do not make your contribution more informative than is required.

Quality: try to make your contribution one that is true

1   Do not say what you believe to be false.
2   Do not say that for which you lack adequate evidence.

Relation

1   Be relevant.

Manner: be perspicuous

1   Avoid obscurity of expression.
2   Avoid ambiguity.
3   Be brief (avoid unnecessary prolixity).
4   Be orderly.

Grice argued that these maxims aren't actually specific to language; if you ask me for a hammer and I hand you a sandwich, I've violated some understood maxim of Relation, because my action is irrelevant to your request. And if you ask for a hammer and I hand you a hammer, a screwdriver, a wrench, and a pile of nails, I've violated the maxim of Quantity.

These aren't particularly surprising maxims; it's not a shock to learn that interlocutors (i.e., people conversing with each other) try to be cooperative, to say the right amount, to say what they believe is true, etc. Where the CP really shines is in its ability to explain how we get from what is said (semantically) to what is meant (in context, i.e., pragmatically). To explain how this works, we need to look at five options speakers have with respect to a maxim: You may **fulfill** it, or you may fail to fulfill it in one of four ways: by quietly **violating** it, by **flouting** it, by negotiating a **clash** between two maxims, or by **opting out** altogether. To opt out is to make it clear that you're not being cooperative: For example, you can respond to a question by saying *I'm sorry; I can't answer that*, or you can simply walk out of the room. In negotiating a clash between maxims, you essentially have to choose which one to prioritize over the other. For instance, it may not be possible to be as informative as is required (Quantity-1) without saying something for which you lack adequate evidence (Quality-2), so perhaps you'll prioritize Quality and say less than is called for. A simple example would be the exchange in (2):

(2) Amy: How did you do on the exam?
    Brad: I think I passed.

In a situation where Brad hasn't yet received his exam grade, his response here represents the most he can say without giving more information than he has evidence for, so he prioritizes limiting his response to such information over giving the most informative response that would be relevant (such as an actual percentage or letter grade). Because Amy knows that the most informative possible response would be a specific grade, and because she knows that Brad also knows this and is trying to be cooperative, she'll understand that he has given the most informative response possible within the constraints of Quality, and will infer that he doesn't know anything more specific about his grade. (Notice that if Brad knows for a fact that he's received an A, his response in (2) is still true, but is now uncooperative and hence misleading.)

In giving a response that conveys more than what he has literally said, Brad has **implicated** the additional meaning – that he doesn't know his exact grade yet. A bit of terminology: In linguistics, to **imply** is like entailment; it leads to a logically valid conclusion. To implicate is more like the layperson's sense of 'imply'; it's a suggestion that isn't stated outright but can be **inferred** from what the speaker has said. The speaker implicates; the hearer infers. What is implied (i.e., logically entailed) is an **implication**; what is implicated is an **implicature**. It can be confusing that what is implicated is NOT an implication, and that what most people think of as implying is what linguists call implicating. But you get used to it. In pragmatics we'll be using the concepts of implicating, implicature, and inference.

Implicatures can arise not only by a speaker negotiating a maxim clash, but also by a speaker fulfilling, flouting, or violating a maxim. When the speaker fulfills or flouts a maxim, the implicature is cooperative; when the speaker violates a maxim, the implicature will be misleading. To see how this works, let's look at each of the maxims individually.

First, the maxim of Quantity tells us to make our contribution as informative as required, but no more so. Consider (3):

(3) Carlos: Who ate all of the pizza?
    Duane: I had some of it.

Here, Duane implicates that he did not eat all of the pizza. Because cooperativity requires him to be as informative as required, if he has in fact eaten all of the pizza, he should say so. Since *some* falls short of *all*, Carlos can infer that *all* doesn't hold. In this case, Duane has fulfilled the requirements of the maxim of Quantity, and Carlos depends on that assumption for his inference. The implicature in this case is called a **scalar implicature**, and reflects a general class of implicatures. The scales that are involved are called **Horn scales** (from Horn 1972) and reflect an ordering from the most informative to the least informative expression, with use of a more informative expression entailing that all less informative expressions hold but implicating that no more informative expression holds.

So in (3), <all, most, some> form a Horn scale: eating *all* of the pizza entails eating *some* of the pizza and eating *most* of the pizza, whereas saying that I ate *some* of the pizza implicates (but does not entail!) that I did not eat *all* or even *most* of the pizza. If in fact I've eaten all of the pizza, saying that I ate some of it is not false, but it is misleading. In that case, I've violated Quantity, and by implicating that I haven't eaten all of the pizza, I've misled my hearer. Brad's implicature in (2) is likewise a scalar implicature; <know, think> form a scale, with *know* entailing *think*, while saying *I think* implicates that I don't know. Other Horn scales include the set of integers, <cold, cool>, and <certain, probable, possible>.

Most relevantly for Grice's purposes, <and, or> form a Horn scale: If (4a) is true, (4b) is necessarily true:

(4) a   Esmeralda had cake and ice cream.
    b   Esmeralda had cake or ice cream.

This explains why *or* can be logically and semantically inclusive (that is, if both *p* and *q* are true, *p or q* is true) yet generally understood as exclusive when used in natural language (that is, uttering *p or q* will implicate that *p and q* is either false or unknown). If (4a) is true, and the speaker knows it to be true, the maxim of Quantity requires them to say (4a) rather than the less informative (4b). By scalar implicature, uttering (4b) will convey that the speaker was not in a position to truthfully utter (4a). Thus, the maxim of Quantity explains a key difference between the semantics of the logical connective *or* and its use in natural language. For Grice, this is a major victory: He has succeeded in his goal of showing how the connectives retain their logical meanings in their natural-language use, with the CP explaining how this logical meaning, combined with the context of utterance, results in the usual understanding. Similar CP-based explanations exist for other discrepancies between logical and natural uses of connectives (e.g., from logical *and* to meanings of ordering or causation, and from logical *if* to a meaning of 'if and only if').

The context of utterance is a crucial participant in this inferential process. For example, as noted above, the scale of integers is a Horn scale, and so choosing a number from the scale will implicate that no higher number holds. If I say *Felix has a cat*, I will generally implicate that Felix has no more than one cat. But in some contexts this implicature doesn't arise:

(5) Greg: It's great that Felix will host the party, but some people have allergies. Does he have a cat?
    Hannah: Yes, he does.
(6) Inez: To get into the bar, we all have to be 21.
    Juan: No worries; I'm 21.

If Felix has two cats, nobody would accuse Hannah in (5) of being misleading, since all that matters in the context is whether Felix has any cats at all. Likewise, in (6) if Juan is actually 22 he hasn't lied, since all that's relevant is whether he's **at least** 21. And of course in having a policy that everybody must be 21 to enter, the bar isn't requiring that everybody be exactly 21; such a bar would soon go out of business. In this case, saying that someone is 21 is as informative as required, and hence fulfills the maxim of Quantity.

One can violate the maxim, as we saw above, by choosing a lower expression on the scale, such as saying you ate some of the pizza when you in fact ate all of it. Because the hearer expects you to be cooperative, they will believe you to have been as informative as required, and will wrongly infer that you did not eat all of it.

More interesting is the notion of flouting a maxim. Here the speaker again fails to fulfill the maxim, but in this case the failure is so blatant that the speaker expects the hearer to realize both that the maxim isn't being satisfied and that they're being expected to notice and to draw the appropriate inference. In the spirit of one of Grice's examples, let's imagine that a student has asked me to write a letter of recommendation for them for a job, and I write the following:

(7) To Whom It May Concern:

My student Kiki Lehrenstein has asked me to write a letter of recommendation for a position with your company. I am pleased to report that Kiki attended class regularly and has excellent penmanship.

Yours sincerely,
Prof. Betty J. Birner

Will I be surprised when Kiki fails to get the job? Of course not. In fact, I've virtually guaranteed that she won't. (This, by the way, is why you should always ask professors whether they can write you a **strong** letter of recommendation, not simply whether they're willing to write a letter of recommendation.) This is what's colloquially known as 'damning with faint praise'. When the situation calls for strong praise, as with a letter of recommendation, a letter that gives vastly less than that – a letter which, for example, omits any mention of the applicant's intelligence, drive, competence, and so on – will so blatantly fail to satisfy the maxim of Quantity that the reader will recognize the failure, and moreover will recognize the writer's intention that they recognize it. Here, in the face of a blatant flouting of Quantity, the reader's belief in the writer's ultimate cooperativity will lead them to seek an alternative explanation for the apparently uncooperative letter, and the best explanation is that there is nothing more that the writer could have said that was positive.

The maxim of Quality tells us not to say anything that we think is false or for which we lack adequate evidence. It can't simply tell us to say what's true, since we can always be wrong about what we believe is true. Because our hearer believes that we're fulfilling this maxim, they will draw the inference that what we say is true (or at least that we think it is). This is a pretty straightforward and, in a sense, uninteresting implicature, but it's obviously crucial to everyday conversation; if you didn't assume that I believed the things I told you, our conversation (and doubtless our relationship) would end quickly. More interesting are quiet violations and floutings of the maxim. A quiet violation of Quality is a lie; I'm saying what I believe to be false or lack evidence for. If our friend Brad in (2) tells Amy that he got 100% on the test without any evidence that this is the case, he has lied – even if it later turns out that he did in fact get 100%. (Though people's intuition about this varies; see Coleman and Kay's (1981) fascinating study of what the word *lie* means.)

As for flouting the maxim, it might initially seem odd to think that anyone would ever want to say something that's blatantly false, but in fact we do it all the time. Blatant falsities include irony, sarcasm, metaphor, metonymy, and hyperbole:

(8) a   [during a raging snowstorm] Well, another lovely Chicago day.

b   [sarcastically] He's quite the Einstein.
c   You're walking a fine line here.
d   I'm parked on Fifth Avenue.
e   I ate a ton of candy this afternoon.

In most contexts, none of these utterances are literally true: A raging snowstorm does not count as a lovely day; the referent in (8b) is not Einstein and probably not even intelligent; most uses of (8c) don't involve any walking or any lines; the speaker in (8d) probably isn't parked anywhere, although their car is; and it's not humanly possible to eat a ton of candy in an afternoon. But in each case, the overarching assumption of the speaker's cooperativity leads the hearer to assume there is some intended meaning that is true, even if the literal meaning isn't. This assumption combines with the context to guide the hearer in coming to the right interpretation.

The maxim of Relation simply says "be relevant," and for this reason many people inaccurately call it the maxim of Relevance. The words' meanings are of course similar; to be relevant is to be related to what has come before. When a speaker fulfills this maxim, the hearer can use the assumption of relevance to infer the relationship between the current utterance and the prior context:

(9) Marty: We're heading to lunch; would you like to come along?
     Norma: I'm on my way to a dentist's appointment.
(10) Olive: Oh no – I forgot to bring my lunch today.
     Pierre: There's a deli around the corner.

In (9), Marty's assumption that Norma is trying to be relevant will lead him to infer that her dentist appointment will prevent her from joining them for lunch. In (10), Pierre implicates that the deli around the corner is relevant to Olive's failure to bring her lunch, and hence that she might consider buying lunch at the deli. In both of these cases, the speaker has fulfilled the maxim of Relation and thereby implicated something beyond what they have said.

To flout Relation is to be so blatantly irrelevant as to give rise to an implicature. For example, our recommendation-writer in (7) above, instead of being simply uninformative, could instead choose to address matters irrelevant to the job, such as the applicant's tennis swing, excellent taste in shoes, fondness for sharp cheeses, etc., and have the same effect. Alternatively, a speaker can flout the maxim of Relation to implicate a pressing need to change the subject:

(11) Quincy: That professor gave the worst lecture I've ever heard! What a moron.
Ramon: Um, nice weather we're having, isn't it?

Here, Ramon implicates a need to discontinue Quincy's topic, which in turn, depending on the context, could implicate disagreement with Quincy's assessment, distaste for insulting one's professors, or a realization that the professor in question is within earshot.

Interestingly, you can use quiet violations of Relation to mislead your hearer without being 'technically' guilty of lying. Consider (12):

(12) Serena: What's up with Therese? I haven't seen her all week.
Ursula: Well, remember Vince said he has a new girlfriend.

Ursula here seems to implicate that Therese is Vince's new girlfriend and that's why she hasn't been around. Now suppose Ursula knows perfectly well that Therese has been on vacation in Europe all week and has never even met Vince. Now her implicature is purposefully misleading. She may have her reasons for wanting to mislead Serena in this way, but if Serena later accuses her of lying, she can respond that she never actually **said** that Vince and Therese were seeing each other.

This points to one big difference between **saying** something and **implicating** it: An implicature is **defeasible**: It can be defeated, or cancelled, whereas something that has been said or entailed cannot. So imagine each of the following as Ursula's response above:

(13) a Well, remember Vince said he has a new girlfriend – but I doubt it's Therese.
b #Well, remember Vince said he has a new girlfriend – but he didn't say he has a new girlfriend.

Hearing (13a), Serena might wonder why Ursula raised the issue of Vince's girlfriend at all, but there are any number of ways in which Ursula might go on to clarify this (. . . *Let me find out whether either of them has seen her*). The important thing is that the implicature can easily be cancelled, whereas what has been explicitly said cannot, as seen in (13b). This property of cancellability holds for conversational implicature in general, as seen for the scalar implicature in (14):

(14) Some, and in fact all, of the children had eaten breakfast.

Here the usual scalar implicature associated with *some* ('not all') is cancelled by the phrase *and in fact all.*

The maxim of Manner is a bit of a grab-bag. It enjoins us to "be perspicuous," and has the sub-maxims "avoid obscurity of expression," "avoid ambiguity," "be brief (avoid unnecessary prolixity)," and "be orderly." All of these are ways of being as clear as possible. (There's an argument to be made that by expanding "be brief" into the not-at-all-brief "avoid unnecessary prolixity" Grice was indulging in a bit of humor.) It's the maxim of Manner that explains the ordering relation frequently associated with *and.* Recall our recipe example in (1b) above, repeated here as (15):

(15) Form the dough into a ball and allow it to rise for two hours.

Here the reader is licensed to infer that the dough should be formed into a ball first, before being allowed to rise for two hours. Imagine an otherwise identical recipe with the following instruction instead:

(16) Allow the dough to rise for two hours and form it into a ball.

Here the reader would be licensed to infer that the dough should rise before being formed into a ball. It would simply be unnecessarily confusing to list the steps in a different order from that in which they should be performed, and hence uncooperative. Even if the recipe explicitly flags the fact that the listed order differs from the order in which the steps should be performed, the reader would be justified in being annoyed:

(17) Allow the dough to rise for two hours, but first form it into a ball.

Here the word *first* cancels the implicature of ordering, so it's not uncooperative in the sense of being misleading, but it would be much more orderly to simply list the steps in the order in which they should occur. And putting the steps in the wrong order with no indication that you're doing so is indeed uncooperative; it constitutes a quiet violation and is hence misleading and will result in many loaves of failed bread.

Cases in which Manner is flouted are perhaps less common than for the other maxims – after all, what purpose is served by a speaker being blatantly unclear? – but one context in which this occurs is when the speaker wants to convey to the hearer that the communicated content is to be kept from some third party. For example, parents will sometimes spell out words in front of a child when they don't want the child to understand what's being said; the implicature here is that the child is not to know what's being discussed.

Thus, the theory of implicature allowed Grice to account for the discrepancies between the logical meanings of the connectives and their use in natural language: Exclusive *or* is a common result of the use of inclusive *or* in combination with the Quantity-based assumption that the speaker is saying as much as they truthfully can (so if *p* and *q* were both true, the speaker should have conveyed that by saying *and* rather than *or*); the ordering associated with *and* is a common result of the maxim of Manner in combination with a context in which ordering is relevant; the causation commonly associated with *and* in *Adele landed an important client and was given a sizeable bonus* is the result of Relation in combination with the context (why mention landing a client if it's not relevant to the bonus?), and so on.

More generally, though, it explains a great deal of the difference between what we say and what we're understood to have intended – and thus bridges the gap between what is said and what is meant, i.e., between semantics and pragmatics. It also explains a fair amount of miscommunication: Because conversational implicature is non-conventional (and thus varies by context), and because it is, in Grice's terms, **calculable** (therefore, reasonable people may differ in what they calculate to be the intended implicature), it will often be the case that what the speaker intends and what the hearer infers will be two different things. Recall our discussion of Reddy's Conduit Metaphor in Chapter 2: Part of what guides our interpretation of non-conventional meaning will be our own internal model of the world, and since each person's model of the world differs, we can't help but occasionally come up with an interpretation of a speaker's utterance that's different from the one they intended.

Pragmatics and reference

We considered in Chapter 2 the question of what exactly a speaker refers to when they use a noun phrase like *the woman in the blue coat* or even *garbanzo beans* – are they referring to some real-world woman or something in their mental model of the world? Are they referring to actual garbanzo beans or to what they believe garbanzo beans to be? If it's something in the real world, how accurate does your description of the real-world object need to be before it no longer refers to that object? What if you think it's accurate and your hearer thinks it's accurate, but it actually isn't and neither of you ever realizes it? Suppose you refer to *the woman in the blue coat* but it's actually a blue dress that looks kind of like a coat; if neither you nor the hearer ever discovers the difference, does it make any sense to say you didn't actually refer to the intended woman?

As we saw then (and are seeing again now), reference can be an extremely thorny issue. And it's also a pragmatic issue, because the hearer has to draw an inference to determine what real-world object the speaker intends to designate. Consider the examples in (18):

(18) a Frederick Douglass was a nineteenth-century abolitionist.
     b The President will deliver the keynote speech this afternoon.
     c She is a renowned physicist.

In (18a), the proper name *Frederick Douglass* designates precisely one individual in the model. Of course, it's certainly possible for two people to have the same name, so this is a bit of an idealization, and strictly speaking an inference is still required to decide that the speaker is referring to the particular Frederick Douglass that I think they're referring to, but for most proper names in most contexts this is a trivial inference to make.

In (18b), *the President* requires a slightly less trivial inference, since there are more presidents of organizations and nations in the world than there are people named Frederick Douglass. But in the vast majority of cases, the context will make the referent clear: If our

Garden Club is meeting today, *the President* probably refers to the President of the Garden Club. If (18b) is uttered at the annual meeting of the Linguistic Society of America, it will be taken to refer to the President of the LSA. And if (18b) is uttered at a national political convention, it will probably be taken to refer to the President of the United States.

It may seem more obvious that an inference is required to determine the referent of *she* in (18c), since female physicists are even more numerous than presidents. And since the speaker in (18c) could be wrong about the referent being a physicist, semantically the noun phrase could be used for anybody or anything that could properly be referred to as *she*. Of course, context once again typically saves the day by providing an obvious target for the reference, but this process is open to ambiguity:

(19) I see Wilma over there talking to Xena. She's a renowned physicist.

Here, the referent of *she* isn't at all clear; it could be either Wilma or Xena. This leads to a bit of a problem for the theory of meaning as we've presented it so far. Suppose we took a straightforward two-stage view of meaning in which the hearer first determines the truth-conditional semantic meaning of the sentence, and then feeds that into the context to decide, using pragmatic principles (such as the CP), the speaker's likely intended meaning. So in (18a), the truth-conditions of *Frederick Douglass was a nineteenth-century abolitionist* would be determined (so the sentence is true if and only if the person designated by the name *Frederick Douglass* was in fact a nineteenth-century abolitionist), and that meaning in combination with the context in which it was uttered would determine any implicatures the speaker may have intended in addition to that semantic meaning. For example, if (18a) immediately followed a previous speaker's comment suggesting that Douglass is doing a good job, the speaker might be taken to implicate that in fact Douglass could not be doing a good job because he is no longer alive.

This (admittedly simplified) process doesn't work in (19). Suppose Wilma is a renowned physicist, but Xena is not. In this case, the sentence is true under the reading in which *she* refers to Wilma, but false on the reading in which *she* refers to Xena. That means that we have to determine the referent of *she* before we can calculate the truth-value of the sentence – and since determining the referent of *she* is a pragmatic process that involves considering the context and the speaker's probable intended meaning, this means that at least some of the pragmatics must happen before the truth of the sentence can be determined. So in interpreting the meaning of an utterance, a hearer will have to consider semantic and pragmatic factors either in tandem or in an interleaved fashion. There are a number of theories that have arisen to address this concern (as we'll see in the next chapter), and researchers are still working to determine the process and order in which speakers work out various aspects of linguistic meaning.

In short, there are still quite a few questions that remain to be answered in the area of reference, and we can only touch on a couple of them here. We looked at some of these issues in Chapter 2, and we'll consider some others below in the section on presupposition. For now, one very intriguing unresolved question worth mentioning is the meaning of the definite article in English – i.e., the word *the*. The question of when it's appropriate to use the word *the* is a remarkably complicated one. For this reason, it's also one of the toughest aspects of English for a non-native speaker to master. The fact that native speakers agree so completely about when it's appropriate to use *the* is a testament to the amazing ability of a child to acquire a native language. It also speaks to the difference between our implicit linguistic competence and our much more limited explicit knowledge: What we know implicitly and use on a day-to-day basis without giving it a moment's thought vastly outstrips what we are able to explain. In the case of *the*, even linguistics researchers have a hard time explaining the rules for its use.

The use of the definite article is an issue of pragmatics, since what determines the choice between the definite and the indefinite is quint-essentially a matter of context:

(20) a   I hear the dog barking.
    b   I hear a dog barking.

The use of the definite in (20a) suggests that the dog in question is familiar, and this is the form you would choose if, for example, the dog that's barking is your own. In (20b), the use of the indefinite suggests that the dog in question is unfamiliar. But 'familiar' and 'unfamiliar' are unsatisfactory characterizations of the use of these forms. For one thing – familiar to whom? It's clearly not enough for the speaker alone to know the referent. For example, (21) would be an odd thing to say if your hearer has no idea who you're talking about:

(21) The guy really annoyed me.

On the other hand, it doesn't seem necessary that your hearer know the precise identity of the referent, since (22) is fine:

(22) The guy who sat next to me on the train this morning really annoyed me.

It seems enough here that the NP *the guy who sat next to me on the train this morning* picks out a unique referent. But is even that necessary? For example, (22) would be acceptable even if the speaker sat between two guys on the train, only one of whom was annoying. But we can't extend this non-uniqueness very far:

(23) #The guy on the train this morning really annoyed me.

Assuming that the train in question usually has any number of people on it, and the hearer has no reason to consider any one of them especially salient, (23) is a very odd thing to say. Instead, the speaker is likely to use an indefinite:

(24) A guy on the train this morning really annoyed me.

The top two pragmatic theories of definiteness, in fact, appeal to these two competing properties: familiarity and uniqueness. In general, if a referent is both familiar (to both speaker and hearer) and uniquely identifiable, the definite will be appropriate, whereas if it is neither familiar nor uniquely identifiable, the indefinite will be appropriate:

(25) a   A car hit the mailbox today.
      b   The car hit a mailbox today.

In (25a), the most likely interpretation is that the car in question is unfamiliar to the hearer and cannot be uniquely identified by them, whereas the mailbox is a uniquely identifiable one known to both speaker and hearer (probably because they own it). In (25b), these characteristics are reversed: The interpretation is likely to be that the car in question is uniquely familiar to the speaker and hearer, while the mailbox is not.

The problem is that neither of these properties is either necessary or sufficient. There are felicitous (i.e., pragmatically appropriate) uses of the word *the* in cases where the referent is unique but not familiar, and there are equally felicitous uses in cases where the referent is familiar but not unique:

(26) a   The oldest living person on earth is 117.
     b   I'm planning to refinish the rocking chair in my bedroom.
     c   Have you seen the Monet in the next gallery?
(27) a   Please pass the salt.
     b   It's stuffy in here; could you open the window?
     c   Take the elevator to the 12th floor.

In (26a), *the oldest living person on earth* needn't be familiar to either the speaker or the hearer; it's sufficient that the NP uniquely picks out this person from all others. In (26b), the hearer needn't have known that the speaker has a rocking chair in their bedroom; they'll simply assume that such a chair exists (see the next section for more on this process) and allow the conversation to continue. And in (26c), the hearer again needn't have known that there was a Monet in the next gallery; as long as there's only one, its status as the unique Monet in the next gallery makes the reference felicitous. In all of these cases, the referent is unique but not familiar to the hearer.

In (27), on the other hand, all three examples illustrate cases in which the referent is familiar to the hearer but not unique. In (27a), even if there are three or four salt shakers on the table visible to the hearer, the definite is felicitous (and certainly doesn't convey that the hearer is to pass all of them). In (27b), even if there are several windows in the room, the definite can felicitously be used to request that one of them be opened – and it doesn't matter which. And finally, in (27c), there can be several elevators available, and again it doesn't matter which one the hearer chooses; nonetheless, the definite is felicitous. In fact, it's somewhat odder to say *Take an elevator to the 12th floor* when the choice of elevator is completely irrelevant.

There are even cases in which it seems a definite is felicitous when the referent is neither familiar nor unique:

(28) a   My cousin is in the hospital.
     b   The fastest way to get downtown is to take the train.
     c   On our trip to Italy, I took a beautiful picture of the mountains.

In (28a), *the hospital* refers to neither a unique nor a known hospital; indeed, in British English the phrase would be *in hospital.* Interestingly, the phrase *in the hospital* as used here carries an additional meaning that the cousin is there as a patient; if they're there, say, doing electrical work, the speaker would be more likely to say the cousin is *at the hospital*, and in that case we'd be more likely to assume the hearer knows which hospital is intended, or that it's a uniquely identifiable or inferrable hospital (such as the nearest local hospital). If there's no such known or identifiable hospital, *My cousin is at the hospital* is more appropriate for a case in which the cousin is there visiting a patient. In short, the difference between *in* and *at* here corresponds to the difference between being a patient and not being a patient, while the use of the definite in the absence of either familiarity or uniqueness suggests that what's being referred to isn't so much a particular hospital as the use of a hospital for its characteristic purpose of health care.

In (28b), *the train* doesn't mean any particular train – neither a known train nor a unique train – but rather any one of a potentially large number of trains that regularly travel back and forth to the downtown area. Similarly to *the hospital*, not only does it here not signal the need for the referent to be known or identifiable, but on the contrary, it seems to signal the complete irrelevance of the identifiability of the particular referent; it seems to be saying that it's the category rather than the particular member of the category that matters.

Finally, in (28c), it's understood by the hearer that the particular set of mountains in the photo are neither unique (there are other mountains in Italy that don't appear in the picture) nor identifiable (there's no indication of which of the various mountains of Italy are in the photo). It's perhaps less clear in this case that which mountains are in the photo is utterly irrelevant, as in the case of the hospital and the train – but even if you're on the point of saying that what the definite marks is the irrelevance of the particular referent, recall that an utterance like (29a) is completely out for an unfamiliar mouse, despite the irrelevance of this particular mouse's identity:

(29) a Yikes! #I just saw the mouse in the kitchen!
    b Yikes! I just saw a mouse in the kitchen!

As a way of conveying that a random entity of the 'mouse' category has shown up in the kitchen, (29a) fails; instead, the indefinite is called for, as in (29b). The use of (29a) strongly conveys that the mouse in question is known – for example, because it's the family's pet mouse, or a particular mouse that keeps getting spotted but then escaping under the fridge, etc.

In short, the use of the definite is one of the most intriguing puzzles in English usage. We've only touched on some of the problems raised by its complex set of uses here, but the principles involved in its use seem to include familiarity, identifiability, uniqueness, exhaustiveness (*give me the red squares* generally is interpreted as 'give me all of the red squares'), characteristic properties, and doubtless more. It's no wonder that non-native learners of English have trouble knowing in a given instance whether they should choose the definite or the indefinite article.

Presupposition

One wrinkle in the use of the definite article is that it's one of a number of expressions in English that can mark a referent as **presupposed**. Precisely what it means for something to be presupposed is controversial, but as a rough first pass, we can say that what's presupposed is taken for granted by the interlocutors. Consider the sentences in (30):

(30) a The King of France is bald.
    b I regret that I voted for the referendum.
    c Yolanda has stopped eating meat.

In (30a), taken from seminal work by Russell (1905) and Strawson (1950), the existence of a King of France is presupposed by the use of the definite. In (30b), the use of the verb *regret* presupposes that its complement – *I voted for the referendum* – is true. (Compare with the use of a non-factive verb as in *I think that I voted for the referendum*, in which one might wonder about the competence of the voter in question but wouldn't take the complement to necessarily be true.) And in (30c), the verb *stopped* presupposes that its complement once held – i.e., that Yolanda previously ate meat. Definites like that in (30a), **factive** verbs taking a presupposed embedded sentence as their complement as in (30b), and **change-of-state** verbs like that in (30c) are all **presupposition triggers**, in that they cue the hearer to the presence of a presupposition.

What a sentence presupposes is different from what it entails. The easiest way to tell the difference is to negate the main verb of the sentence. When the sentence is negated, the presupposition remains unaffected:

(31) a   The King of France is not bald.
     b   I do not regret that I voted for the referendum.
     c   Yolanda has not stopped eating meat.

In these negated versions of the sentences in (30), the presuppositions in (32) remain intact:

(32) a   There is a King of France.
     b   I voted for the referendum.
     c   Yolanda has previously eaten meat.

Compare these with the sentences in (33), which entail the propositions in (34):

(33) a   France is a country in Europe.
     b   I voted for the referendum.
     c   Yolanda had steak for dinner.
(34) a   France is a country.
     b   I voted.
     c   Yolanda had meat for dinner.

Negating the sentences in (33), as in (35), does not preserve the entailments in (34):

(35) a   France is not a country in Europe.
     b   I did not vote for the referendum.
     c   Yolanda did not have steak for dinner.

That is, (35a) does not entail that France is a country, (35b) does not entail that I voted, and (35c) does not entail that Yolanda had meat for dinner.

Thus, a reliable test for presupposition is **constancy under negation** – the fact that a sentence and its negation share presuppositions.

Although negating a sentence does not preserve its entailments, negating an entailment negates the entailing sentence. So because the sentences in (33) entail the corresponding sentences in (34), the negated versions of (34) seen in the (a) sentences below entail the negated versions of (33) seen in the (b) sentences:

(36) a   France is not a country.
     b   France is not a country in Europe.
(37) a   I did not vote.
     b   I did not vote for the referendum.
(38) a   Yolanda did not have meat for dinner.
     b   Yolanda did not have steak for dinner.

To put it another way, if *France is a country in Europe* entails that France is a country, then if France isn't a country, it can't be a country in Europe – and similarly for (37) and (38).

Again, presupposition differs on this front. If you negate the presupposition, it's not clear what the effect is on the sentence that presupposes it. That is, if the (b) sentences in (39)–(41) are false, what is the status of the (a) sentences?

(39) a   The King of France is bald.
     b   There is a King of France.
(40) a   I regret that I voted for the referendum.
     b   I voted for the referendum.
(41) a   Yolanda has stopped eating meat.
     b   Yolanda has previously eaten meat.

If there's no King of France, is the sentence *The King of France is bald* true, false, both, neither, or something else altogether? And we can ask the same question of *I regret that I voted for the referendum* if in fact I didn't vote for the referendum, and of *Yolanda has stopped eating meat* if Yolanda has never before eaten meat.

Philosophers of language have been divided on this question, with some arguing that if the presupposition is false, any sentence presupposing it is false; others arguing that the presupposing sentence lacks a truth-value; and still others arguing that the falsity of the presupposition simply renders the presupposing sentence inappropriate (why are we talking about the King's hairlessness if there's no King?) or otherwise infelicitous. By now you'll recognize the first two approaches, based on truth-values, as semantic in nature (at least for those who define semantic meaning as any aspect of meaning that affects truth-conditions), while those that take the problem to lie in inappropriateness or infelicity are pragmatic in nature. You might also note that if we're going to say that the presupposing sentence lacks a truth-value – that it's neither true nor false – we'll need to expand our currently **bivalent** system of two truth-values (true and false) into a **multivalent** system in which there exists (at least) a third option beyond those two options.

Russell (1905) argued that if there's no King of France, *The King of France is bald* is simply false. In his view, the semantics of this sentence are as shown in (42).

(42) $\exists x((K(x) \land \forall y(K(y) \rightarrow y=x)) \land B(x))$

Remember this notation from Chapter 2? If we take K to represent 'King of France' and B to represent 'bald' and '=' to represent identity, this means essentially, 'there exists something such that it's the King of France and such that anything that's the King of France is that thing; and that thing is bald'. Or, more simply, 'there is one and only one King of France, and he is bald'. In this view, if any of the following are true, *The King of France is bald* is false:

(43) a   There is no King of France.
      b   There is more than one King of France.
      c   The King of France is not bald.

Frege (1892), on the other hand, believed that if there's no King of France, *The King of France is bald* is neither true nor false, and Strawson (1950) agreed.

There are several problems with a purely semantic account of presupposition, however. For one thing, under a semantic account, what is presupposed is also entailed; that is, in any case in which *The King of France is bald* is true, *There is a King of France* must also be true, since if it's not true, the sentence that presupposes it will be either false (according to Russell) or truth-valueless (according to Frege and Strawson). And we've already seen that there's a difference between presupposition and entailment: Presuppositions remain constant under negation, whereas entailments in general don't. Consider the fact that (44a) presupposes (44b) but entails (44c):

(44) a   The King of France is bald.
      b   There is a King of France.
      c   Somebody is bald.

Now if you negate (44a) (*The King of France is not bald*), the sentence still presupposes (44b), the existence of a King of France, but it no longer entails (44c), that somebody is bald. Also, entailments generally aren't cancellable, but presuppositions sometimes are:

(45) a   The King of France isn't bald; there is no King of France!
      b   The King of France is bald, if indeed there is a King of France.

The first clause of (45a) – *The King of France isn't bald* – presupposes the existence of a King of France, but the second clause cancels this presupposition. Recall that implicatures (a pragmatic phenomenon) are cancellable, but entailments (a semantic phenomenon) are not. In (45b), what we have isn't technically a cancellation but rather a **suspension** of the presupposition (Horn 1972). The ability to either suspend or cancel the presupposition suggests that it is not the same as an entailment, which can be neither suspended nor cancelled. This argument isn't as strong as we might like, however, since the circumstances in which a presupposition can be cancelled are tightly constrained. For example, you can't readily cancel the presupposition of a positive assertion, as shown in (46):

(46) #The King of France is bald; there is no King of France!

For this reason, some researchers have argued that what we have in (45a) is actually a **metalinguistic negation** in which what's being negated isn't the primary assertion but rather some other linguistic aspect of what was said. You can metalinguistically negate just about any aspect of an utterance, including pronunciation (*I didn't say I wanted the 'cat-sup'; I said I wanted the ketchup.*)

Nonetheless, there are non-metalinguistic utterances in which the usual presupposition associated with a definite does not arise:

(47) The King of France is a fictional notion invoked to make a point about presupposition.

Here, there is no presupposition that the King of France exists. That means that context is a factor in the presence or absence of a presupposition, and that in turn constitutes evidence that presupposition is a pragmatic phenomenon.

One pragmatic approach taken by, e.g., Stalnaker (1974) is to consider the presupposition to be part of the **common ground** of the utterance – that is, the material that the interlocutors take to be shared between them. On this view, if the presupposition isn't true, then the issue of truth or falsity doesn't arise for the presupposing sentence; instead, it's simply an inappropriate or odd thing to say: The problem isn't so much our inability to determine whether a non-existent king is bald or not; the problem is the bizarreness of even raising the question. Only once both interlocutors take the existence of the King of France as a given – or at least uncontroversial – does the question of whether or not he is bald make sense.

But the 'or at least uncontroversial' caveat is important: Not everything that's presupposed is actually part of the prior common ground of the interlocutors. Consider the examples in (48):

(48) a   My brother is a referee.
     b   I have to go home and feed the cat.
     c   I need you to run into the next room and bring me the ruler that's on the desk.
     d   The burger I had for lunch is disagreeing with me.

Each of these presupposes something that needn't be previously known to the addressee for the utterance to be felicitous. These presuppositions are given in (49):

(49) a   I have a brother.
      b   I have a cat.
      c   There's a ruler on the desk in the next room.
      d   I had a burger for lunch.

These have all the hallmarks of presupposition, for example, the crucial property of constancy under negation: *My brother isn't a referee*
still presupposes that I have a brother, *I don't have to go home and
feed the cat* still presupposes that I have a cat, and so on. But none of
these presuppositions need to be part of the common ground shared
by the interlocutors; (48a) is a perfectly fine thing to say to someone
who doesn't know that I have a brother, (48b) is a perfectly reasonable thing to say to someone who doesn't know that I have a cat,
and so on. In these cases, the hearer will simply **accommodate** the
presupposition (Lewis 1979); they'll essentially add a brother, cat,
or whatever to the discourse model just as though it had been there
already, and the conversation will continue. In essence, the hearer
seems to be reasoning that if the speaker is treating the fact that they
have a brother as part of the common ground, it must be the case
that they have a brother. And in that case, it's much more efficient
just to add the brother-of-the-speaker to the discourse model than
to hold up the discourse by saying *Wait – your definite NP presupposes a brother, but you haven't mentioned one. Do you in fact have
a brother?* For something as uncontroversial as having a brother (or a
cat, or a ruler), that would be just silly. It makes sense to challenge the
presupposition only if the speaker is trying to presuppose something
odd, false, or controversial:

(50) a   I have to go home and feed the chinchilla.
      b   Could I borrow your car this afternoon?
      c   The prof's incompetence is ruining this class for me.

Rather than simply accommodating the presuppositions of these utterances, the hearer might choose to challenge or comment on them on
various grounds:

(51) a   Wait – you've got a chinchilla?
      b   I'm sorry; I don't own a car.

    c   You think the prof is incompetent too? Wow, I thought I was the only one.

So, on the one hand, there's reason to believe that presupposition is a pragmatic phenomenon, since it doesn't act like entailment and is affected by context. On the other hand, defining it as whatever is in the common ground is insufficiently nuanced, since we're able to accommodate presuppositions that aren't in the common ground. Yet we also don't yet have an account of precisely when a presupposition can be accommodated and when it cannot. Researchers have approached potential solutions to the problem of presupposition by various routes, including distinguishing between conventional/semantic sources of presupposition and contextual/pragmatic sources, distinguishing between controversial and non-controversial aspects of a proposition, etc. One approach is to distinguish between the **asserted** and the **non-asserted** material in an utterance, with non-asserted material constituting the presupposition (Abbott 2002, 2008). It's also worth noting the close relationship between the problems inherent in dealing with presupposition and those inherent in defining constraints on definiteness, since, as we saw above, definiteness is one of the presupposition triggers. Moreover, if a crucial factor in the use of presupposition is the speaker's intent to distinguish what is being asserted from what is not, we'll need a theory of what exactly it is that a speaker does in making an assertion, and the extent to which their intentions determine this. In short, we'll need a theory of **speech acts**.

Speech acts: getting things done with language

The theory of speech acts has its roots in the work of Austin (1962). At its most basic, it's a theory of what we do when we speak. To speak is to act, both in an obvious sense (you can't speak without performing the action of speaking) and also in a less obvious sense. Austin observed the somewhat surprising fact that certain sentences not only describe an action but also simultaneously perform the action they're describing. To see this, consider the sentences in (52):

(52) a   I bet $10. [e.g., in a poker game]

b   I thank you for your service.
c   I apologize for breaking your favorite vase.

The speaker in (52a) not only describes the bet they are making, but in fact makes the bet by virtue of making the statement: The statement itself serves as the making of the bet. In (52b), the speaker not only describes, but in fact performs, an act of thanking by virtue of making the statement: The statement is itself the thanks. And similarly, in (52c), the speaker, by stating that they are apologizing, in fact apologizes: The statement is itself the apology. Statements such as these, which perform the action they describe, are called **performatives**, and verbs that can be used in this way are **performative verbs**. These can be distinguished from non-performative verbs, which cannot be used in this way:

(53) a   I love to dance.
      b   I teach linguistics.
      c   I regret breaking your favorite vase.

A speaker making the statement in (53a) may be accurately describing how they feel about dancing, but the statement does not in itself perform the act of loving to dance; it doesn't bring about the love of dancing in the same way that (52a) brings about the bet. Similarly, the speaker in (53b) is not, in that utterance, teaching linguistics in the same way that the speaker of (52b) is, in that utterance, thanking someone for their service; and the speaker in (53c) does not regret anything by means of making the statement in the same way that the speaker of (52c) apologizes by means of making that statement. To put it another way, if the sentences in (52) (or their equivalents) are never uttered, the bet hasn't been made, the thanks haven't been offered, and the apology has not been made, whereas if the sentences in (53) are never uttered, it's still entirely possible that the individuals in question love to dance, teach linguistics, and regret breaking the vase, respectively.

So, on the one hand, we have performative utterances, which perform the act they semantically describe. And then we have non-performative utterances, which may semantically describe an act but do not perform it. And on the opposite side of the scale, we have utterances that seem to perform some act other than the one that matches their semantics:

(54) a   I need you to help me lift this.
     b   Can you pass the salt?
     c   I wonder what time it is.
     d   Isn't it a beautiful day?

In (54a), the speaker isn't just describing a need they happen to have; they're making a request. In (54b), the speaker isn't really asking about the hearer's salt-passing abilities; they're again making a request, this time by means of a question rather than a statement. In (54c), the speaker again isn't simply describing their state of mind, but rather asking a question. And finally, in (56d), the speaker isn't actually asking whether it's a beautiful day, but rather asserting that it is.

In each of these instances, the speaker is performing a particular speech act **indirectly**, by means of some other act. In (54a) the speaker uses a statement in order to perform the act of making a request, in (54b) they use a question to perform the act of making a request, in (54c) they use a statement in order to ask a question, and in (54d) they use a question to make a statement. Notice that there are more direct forms conventionally associated with the acts of making a request, asking a question, and making a statement; these are the **imperative**, **interrogative**, and **declarative** forms, respectively, as shown in (55):

(55) a   Help me lift this. [imperative]
     b   Please pass the salt. [imperative]
     c   What time is it? [interrogative]
     d   It's a beautiful day. [declarative]

In the **indirect speech acts** in (54), the form conventionally associated with an act (declarative for statements, interrogative for questions, imperative for requests and commands) is not the one selected for that act; that is, there is technically a mismatch between the form and the function. Nonetheless, the speaker usually has no difficulty getting their meaning across, and here the CP plays a central role. For example, why on earth would the speaker in (54a) be mentioning this need? The maxim of Quantity says they should say no more than is necessary, and the maxim of Relation says their utterances should be relevant; putting these two together, the hearer can infer that by mentioning their need for help in a context in which a request for help would be relevant, they mean to implicate a request. The request needn't be stated explicitly, since mention of the need for help is sufficient to convey the request. Likewise, in (54b) a hearer's salt-passing ability is most relevant if the speaker actually wants them to pass the salt (Relation), and therefore if the speaker wants them to pass the salt, that's all they really need to say to get the deed done (Quantity). Similar explanations apply to the other examples; you can readily work out the details for yourself.

Indeed, it can seem quite abrupt and even a bit rude to simply state a command flat-out:

(56) a   Help me lift this.
    b   Pass the salt.
    c   Lend me $20.
    d   Do the dishes.

The extent to which these are appropriate or rude varies, as always, with context. If two people are already working together on a project, so that requests for help with various parts of the project are normal, (56a) isn't at all an odd way to make the request. On the other hand, if you're trying to pick up, say, a ladder, and someone wanders by just as you find you're having difficulty, you'd never use (56a) or even (54a) to make the request; instead, you'd go with something like (57):

(57) Could you possibly help me lift this?

That is, you wouldn't state the request or even your need for help; you'd ask whether help is possible. Similarly, while (56b) might be a perfectly normal way to request the salt from a close family member, you'd never use it while dining with a prospective employer during a job interview; instead, you'd **hedge** the request with *Could you* or *Might you* or at the very least *Please.* And only a very close friend or family member can get away with (56c) or (56d) as a direct command; for anyone else, you're going to want to add not only a *please* but also *Could you, Could you possibly, Would you be able to, Would you mind, Would it be too much trouble, I'd be grateful if, It would be really helpful if you could . . .*, or something similar.

All of these hedges rely, as it turns out, on preconditions for the requested action – what we call **felicity conditions**. In order for a request to be made felicitously, it's necessary that the person making the request actually wants it to be performed, that (they believe) the person on the receiving end of the request is able to perform it, that (they believe) this person is willing to perform it, and so on. Many indirect requests function by stating or questioning these felicity conditions. Consider some of the felicity conditions on a request listed in (58) and the indirect requests that either state or question them in (59):

(58) Felicity conditions on a request that the hearer do X:

    a X would be helpful.
    b   Speaker would like for hearer to do X.
    c   Hearer is able to do X.
    d   Hearer is willing to do X.

(59) a   It would be really helpful if you did the dishes.
    b   I'd appreciate it if you did the dishes.
    c   Could you do the dishes?
    d   Are you willing to do the dishes?

By either stating or questioning these felicity conditions, the speaker is able to convey, via Relation, that they're hoping the satisfaction of the felicity condition will further lead to the performance of the requested action. And the more felicity conditions are built into the indirect request, the more hedged and polite it becomes:

(60) I'd really appreciate it if you would possibly be willing to help by doing the dishes.

Here the speaker has artfully worked in all four of the felicity conditions in (58): X would be helpful (*to help*), speaker would like hearer to do X (*I'd really appreciate it*), hearer is able to do X (*possibly*), and hearer is willing to do X (*be willing*). Nonetheless, semantically there is nothing here that explicitly requests or commands that the hearer do the dishes, so the hearer is free to decline by countering one of the questioned felicity conditions:

(61) a   I'm sorry, but I'm on my way out the door, so I can't.
      b   Hey, I did them yesterday; it's your turn.

The respondent in (61a) counters their ability to do the dishes, while the respondent in (61b) counters their willingness. Needless to say, it's somewhat more difficult, and thus much less common, for a respondent to try to escape dish duty (or some analogous task) by arguing against the action's usefulness or the speaker's state of mind.

Different performative verbs have different felicity conditions. For example, *promise* differs from *warn* in the expected effect on the listener:

(62) a   I promise to take you for ice cream later.
      b   I warn you, if you keep this up you won't get any ice cream.

In general, both *promise* and *warn* share the felicity conditions that the speaker be able and willing to bring about the mentioned event, but they differ in whether the hearer is believed to want the event to come about or not. For this reason, (63a) has an ironic feel, while (63b) seems to suggest that the hearer dislikes ice cream, and (63c) is simply odd:

(63) a   I promise you, if you keep this up you won't get any ice cream.
      b   I promise not to take you for ice cream.
      c   I warn you, I'm going to take you for ice cream later.

The utterance in (63c) only really works as a warning if there's some contextually known information that's missing here – for example, if the hearer is deathly allergic to milk products, or really needs to get to an appointment that the ice cream outing will make them late for.

Because performatives describe what the speaker is using the utterance to do at the precise moment that they're doing it, they're always in the first person and present tense. So the sentences in (64) are performatives, but the sentences in (65) are not:

(64) a   I promise to take you for ice cream later.
      b   I warn you, if you keep this up you won't get any ice cream.
      c   I beg you not to deny me ice cream.

     d   I bet you 50 cents Mom will take us for ice cream later.

     e   I apologize for not taking you for ice cream.

(65) a   Dad promised to take you for ice cream later.

     b   Dad warns you, if you keep this up you won't get any ice cream.

     c   I begged you not to deny me ice cream.

     d   John bets you 50 cents Mom will take us for ice cream later.

     e   I apologized for not taking you for ice cream.

Although the utterances in (65) might describe someone else's promise, warning, bet, etc., or one that the speaker has previously made, they do not in themselves constitute the described speech act.

Because the act is performed by virtue of the utterance, one good test for a performative is to see whether the word *hereby* can be inserted:

(66) a   I hereby promise to take you for ice cream later.

     b   I hereby warn you, if you keep this up you won't get any ice cream.

     c   I hereby beg you not to deny me ice cream.

     d   I hereby bet you 50 cents Mom takes us for ice cream later.

     e   I hereby apologize for not taking you for ice cream.

(67) a   #Dad hereby promised to take you for ice cream later.

     b   #Dad hereby warns you, if you keep this up you won't get any ice cream.

     c   #I hereby begged you not to deny me ice cream.

     d   #John hereby bets you 50 cents Mom will take us for ice cream later.

     e   #I hereby apologized for not taking you for ice cream.

The performatives in (66) readily admit the addition of *hereby*, whereas the non-performatives in (67) do not. The only exceptions are (67b) and (67d), in which the utterance could act as making a warning or a bet on behalf of Dad or John, respectively, if and only if the speaker is acting as their agent – and in that case, the addition of *hereby* clarifies this agency.

As we've seen, a performative enacts what it semantically describes. A direct speech act performs the act conventionally associated with its form, not with its semantic content:

(68) a   I like ice cream.
      b   Do you like ice cream?
      c   Take me for some ice cream.

The utterance in (68a) performs the act of making a statement by virtue of its declarative form, (68b) performs the act of asking a question by virtue of its interrogative form, and (68c) performs the act of making a request by virtue of its imperative form – but none of these performs the act of liking ice cream or taking the speaker for ice cream.

Finally, an indirect speech act performs an act conventionally associated neither with its form nor with its semantic content; rather, the intended meaning is inferred based on a combination of the semantic content, contextual factors, and the CP, as seen above.

Because the meaning of an indirect speech act must be inferred, it is possible for the speaker's intention and the hearer's inference to differ; that is, the hearer can be wrong about what the speaker intended, as in (69):

(69) Zelda: I wonder how long it will take me to get to the opera house.
     Alvin: Sorry, I don't know where the opera house is.
     Zelda: It's on 95th St. at the corner of Oak, just about a mile north of the freeway.
     Alvin: Okay, but I still don't know how long it would take to get there.

Here, Zelda begins the interaction with an indirect question ('how long will it take me to get to the opera house?'). Zelda takes Alvin's response as an indirect request for information – specifically, where the opera house is. Instead, he intends it as an indirect and polite refusal to speculate on how long it will take to get there. When she tells him where it is, he sees the miscommunication: She thought he was indirectly asking for the location, but he wasn't. So he then has to make his actual meaning – i.e., that he won't venture to guess how long it will take to get there – somewhat more explicit. Note that it's not yet totally explicit; as is so often the case, he cites the failure of a felicity condition (I don't know X) as a way of implicating that he won't be performing the speech act for which it is a felicity condition (I won't tell you X).

Given the potential disconnect between a speaker's intended speech act and the hearer's understanding of what speech act has been performed, we need to distinguish between what has been literally said, what the speaker intended by it, and the effect on the hearer. What has been said is called the **locutionary force** of the utterance. What the speaker intended to do by uttering it is its **illocutionary force**. And, finally, its effect on the hearer is its **perlocutionary force**. For example, Alvin's first utterance in (69) has the locutionary force of a statement (I don't know where the opera house is), the illocutionary force of a refusal (I won't tell you how long it takes to get there), and the perlocutionary force of a request (tell me where it is). A difference between the illocutionary force (i.e., the intended effect) and the perlocutionary force (i.e., the actual effect) is one source of miscommunication.

Meaning and word order

We've seen many ways in which a single sentence with a single semantic meaning can give rise to various understandings when uttered, most recently in our discussion of indirect speech acts. Interestingly, it is also possible for a single semantic meaning to be 'packaged' in a variety of ways as different sentences with the same meaning. Consider, for example, the sentences in (70):

(70) a   The book is lying on the table.
     b   On the table is lying the book.
     c   There is lying the book on the table.
     d   On the table there is lying the book.
     e   There is lying on the table the book.
     f   On the table the book is lying.
     g   On the table, the book is lying there.
     h   What is lying on the table is the book.
     i   It's on the table that the book is lying.
     j   What the book is lying on is the table.
     k   It's the table that the book is lying on.
     l   The table, the book is lying on.
     m   The table is what the book is lying on.
     n   The table is being lain on by the book.

I could go on for quite a while with additional, ever more strained but fully grammatical variants. Why on earth does language give us so many ways of saying the same thing, and what makes some of them seem more strained? The truly interesting thing, from the perspective of conveying meaning, is that in some contexts even the most strained examples become flawless:

(71)   Beverly has arranged her room so that everything in it is lying on top of something else. We're not sure why, but she's a little odd that way. In any case, I'm sure you'll want to know what is on top of what. Her bracelet is lying on an envelope, which in turn is lying on a book. What the book is lying on is the table.

The crucial thing for the felicity of (70j), as it turns out, is that *the book* be contrasted with other items in the frame '*X* is lying on *Y*'. So as long as we've set up a scenario in which a bunch of things are lying on other things, and one of the things lying on other things is a familiar or previously mentioned book (to license the definite article), we're in business. The syntactic construction in (70j) is called a *wh*-**cleft**, in contrast to the *it*-**cleft** in (70k). Both of them serve to pull out one element of the sentence and focus on it as the answer to some implicit question – here, the question 'what is the book lying on?' So for felicitous use of either of these constructions, we need two things to be **salient**, i.e., either evoked in the prior discourse, inferrable based on it, or otherwise 'in the air' between the interlocutors: the proposition '*X* is lying on *Y*' and sets of candidates for filling in *X* and *Y*. In short, what determines when you can use a particular syntactic construction is – no surprise here – the context.

To see this more clearly, consider the construction in (70b), known as **inversion**. In an inversion, what would normally be the subject in the default, or **canonical**, word order gets moved to the back of the sentence while something that's canonically at the back gets moved to the front. Compare (72a) and (72b):

(72)   a   Charlene owns an amazing fish tank. Seven enormous piranha live in the fish tank.
         b   Charlene owns an amazing fish tank. In the fish tank live seven enormous piranha.

    c   Charlene owns seven enormous piranha. #In an amazing fish tank live the piranha.

In (72a), the second sentence is in canonical word order. Different languages have different canonical word orders; in English, the canonical order is subject-verb-object. The category 'object' should really be called 'complement'; recall from Chapter 3 that the verb essentially selects its complements, and *live* selects a prepositional phrase complement (describing where the subject lives) rather a noun phrase complement. So the canonical word order for an English sentence with the verb *live* is subject-*live*-PP, as in *Seven enormous piranha live in the fish tank*. In the inversion in (72b), the subject *seven enormous piranha* gets placed at the back of the sentence, and the PP *in the fish tank* gets moved to the front.

    In (72c), we've got another inversion, but we've changed the context. Notice that in (72b) the fish tank that's been moved to the front (**preposed**) is already under discussion, whereas in (72c) the piranha that have been moved to the back (**postposed**) are already under discussion. And we see that the inversion is not felicitous if the preposed phrase is new while the postposed phrase is under discussion.

    This is actually part of a larger pattern: Preposing in general requires the preposed phrase to be already salient in the context (either by having already been mentioned or by standing in a salient set relationship to something that's already been mentioned), whereas postposing in general requires the postposed phrase to be new in some sense – either new to the discourse (**discourse-new**) or, in the case of postposings with *be* as the main verb (called **existential** sentences), new to the hearer (**hearer-new**). Consider the following short discourses, in which the non-canonical sentences are italicized:

(73) a   I like spaghetti, steak, and stir-fries best. *Spaghetti I love.*
      b   I'm not crazy about most Italian food, but *spaghetti I love.*
      c   I enjoy doing woodworking projects. #*Spaghetti I love.*
      d   Italian food tends to be heavy on carbs. #*Spaghetti I love.*
(74) a   I read an interesting magazine yesterday. *In it there were several articles about woodworking.*
      b   I read several articles about woodworking yesterday. #*In an interesting magazine there were the articles.*

    c   I read several articles about woodworking yesterday. #*There were the articles in an interesting magazine.*

In (73), we see that a preposing requires two things: first, that the preposed phrase be either previously mentioned (as in (73a)) or stand in a set relationship to something that's already salient (as with Italian food in (73b)); and, second, that there be a salient **open proposition**. An open proposition, as we saw in Chapter 3, is a proposition in which one or more elements is unspecified; and just like the clefts we looked at above, a preposing requires such a proposition to be salient in the context. So for the felicitous preposings in (73a) and (73b), the initial sentence makes salient the proposition 'I like {foods} to X degree', where the bracketed {foods} indicates the set of foods. In (73c), we've got the salient proposition 'I like X to Y degree' (based on my saying I like woodworking projects), but we lack the set relationship between the information in the prior context and the preposed phrase *spaghetti.* In (73d), we've got that relationship, but we lack the open proposition. In both cases, infelicity results.

    The italicized sentences in (74) are postposings; here, the subject is moved to the end of its clause and then, because English requires a subject, its usual place is occupied by a semantically empty *there* (that is, *there* in this case doesn't mean 'in that place'; in fact, it means nothing at all and is really just a place-holder). Postposed phrases are required to represent new information, such as the articles in (74a). If you change the prior sentence so that the articles are now familiar, as in (74b), the postposing becomes infelicitous. Notice that placing the PP at the end, as in (74c), doesn't help; it's still a postposing, and it's still infelicitous with a familiar postposed phrase, although the canonical variant (*The articles were in an interesting magazine*) is fine in this context.

    In short, only discourse-old information can be preposed, and only new information can be postposed – either discourse-new or hearer-new information, depending on the subtype of postposing. And inversion, which has one preposed and one postposed phrase, requires at least one or the other of these two phrases to adhere to the relevant standard; either the preposed phrase must be familiar or the postposed phrase must be unfamiliar. In this sense, we can think of an inversion as having to satisfy either the constraint on preposing or the constraint on postposing, which is why a felicitous inversion can't combine preposed discourse-new information and postposed discourse-old information, as in (72c).

This answers one of the questions posed at the beginning of this section, which is why some of the examples seem so strained; it's because there are contextual constraints on their use. Only when those contextual requirements are met do the non-canonical constructions feel comfortable. But we still haven't gotten an answer to the other question, which is why language would give us all these options. There are several apparent answers: First, researchers have known for a long time that many languages prefer sentences to be organized in a given-before-new order – that is, with information that is in some sense 'old' appearing earlier in the sentence than information that is in some sense 'new'. This makes good sense, really: Putting the 'given' or old information first helps the hearer to see exactly how it connects to the previous discourse, and in that way provides a sort of hook to attach the new information to, and in turn allows the new information to be focused on at the end of the sentence and take its place as the now-known information for the next sentence.

In general, canonical word order isn't constrained in terms of the givenness or newness of its constituents (what we call their **information status**). But just stringing together canonical-word-order sentences without regard to the information status of their constituents can result in an awkward and hard-to-read discourse:

(75) a   A house was once in the woods. Three bears lived in the house. A little girl happened by one day while the bears were out walking. She went in and saw a table and three chairs. Three bowls of porridge were on the table.

      b   Once there was a house in the woods. In the house lived three bears. One day while the bears were out walking, a little girl happened by. She went in and saw a table and three chairs. On the table were three bowls of porridge.

The discourse in (75a) is hard to read, because the sentences are all constructed in subject-verb-complement order with no regard for the information status of their constituents. The version in (75b) is much easier to read, because the use of non-canonical constructions makes it possible to place familiar information at the beginning of each sentence and new information at the end.

So one reason language gives us so many ways to say the same thing is to allow us to maintain this given-before-new ordering. Another reason is that it helps to tell our hearer what to focus on in the sentence: In general, what's new is also what's interesting about the sentence. So in (75b), even though the first sentence has no 'old' information, it's still helpful to move *a house in the woods* to the end, a place where focused information is conventionally placed, because this placement in itself tells the hearer that this house is the focus of the discourse at the moment. And then in the second sentence, the house essentially 'hands off' the focus to the three bears, who in turn hand it off in the third sentence to the little girl.

Thus, our understanding of a convention like 'new, focused material goes at the end' cues us to interpret the material at the end as new, focused material. And in a similar vein, our understanding of the constraints on non-canonical word orders that require discourse-old information in a certain position will inform our decisions about when a phrase should be taken to be discourse-old, as illustrated in (76):

(76) a   Last night I went out to buy the picnic supplies. I decided to get beer first.

     b   Last night I went out to buy the picnic supplies. Beer I decided to get first.

In (76a), taken from Birner 2006, the second sentence is ambiguous: It could mean that I decided to get beer before starting in on the purchase of picnic supplies, or it could mean that of all the picnic supplies, the first thing I bought was the beer. That is, it's ambiguous between whether the beer is or isn't part of the picnic supplies. This ambiguity vanishes in (76b): Here, the beer is necessarily part of the picnic supplies. Why? Because the hearer knows that preposing requires the preposed phrase to refer to discourse-old information. In (76b), *beer* is preposed; therefore, it must be discourse-old. Since it hasn't been explicitly mentioned in the prior discourse, it must stand in a set relationship to something that has been mentioned, and the only candidate is the picnic supplies. Hence, the beer must be a member of the set of picnic supplies.

So, in a neat twist, speakers can convey information purely by means of the hearer's knowledge that a given structure is conventionally used to convey that information. And, really, this is the way all language works: When I use the word *dog*, it only has meaning to you because you know that I know that you'll interpret it to mean 'dog', and I only use it because I know that you know that I know this, and it's only because you realize that I know that . . . well, you get the idea. Language only works because there exists this mutual and recursive understanding that we're both in this together, and that I only say what I expect you to understand due to our shared conventions, and you only understand it because you know I expect you to. Which, inevitably, brings us back to Grice: Conversation works because it's a cooperative venture.

Chapter 5

Conclusion

This has been a whirlwind tour of linguistic meaning, focusing on some of the primary issues in philosophy of language, semantics, and pragmatics. Needless to say, I haven't been able to touch on everything that's going on in current research, but I do hope to have laid the groundwork so that you can go on to read current work in these areas. My ulterior motive, of course, has been to get you sufficiently interested that you'll decide that you, too, want to devote your career to research in this area and contribute to the ongoing discussion. I can personally attest to the fact that it's a lot of fun!

In this final chapter, I'll point you in the right direction by, first, summarizing what we've covered so far; second, giving you a taste of ongoing controversies in the field; and, finally, presenting some suggestions for further reading.

Summary of foundational issues

We started this book with the question "What is meaning?" There is, of course, no one single answer, but the intervening pages have presented a range of philosophical, semantic, and pragmatic responses to the question of what meaning is and how interlocutors engage in collaborative meaning-making. We've taken a primarily truth-conditional approach to semantic meaning, though there are other approaches one could take as well (see below for a discussion of the issues involved). We've also taken a mostly compositional approach to semantic meaning, though again there are other approaches that are worth your time to look into. Here is a super-quick run-through of what each chapter covered:

Philosophical approaches to meaning

Reddy (1979) argued that a pervasive 'Conduit Metaphor' in English leads its speakers to falsely believe that meaning is something that's effortlessly passed from one speaker to another. Instead, Reddy argues, communication is difficult and requires interlocutors to try to infer each other's intended meanings based on a combination of what has been said, the context, and their beliefs about each other's ultimately unknowable mental world. Reddy's view of the effect of language on our view of communication reflects Whorf's (1941 and elsewhere) view that the language a person speaks influences the way they see reality. Reddy's emphasis on our inability to access a crucial aspect of meaning – the speaker's mental world – also reflects a cognitivist viewpoint, in which referents reside in the minds of speakers and hearers, as opposed to a referentialist viewpoint, in which they reside in the real world. Frege's related distinction between sense and reference distinguishes what is conventional in the meaning of a word or phrase (its sense) from what a speaker picks out by using it (its reference). This distinction helps to explain how two phrases that pick out the same thing in reality might not pick out the same thing for an individual, and so the phrases can't necessarily be swapped in a sentence about a person's propositional attitude without changing the truth-value of the sentence. Another distinction that depends on a person's world view and its relationship to reality is Donnellan's referential/attributive distinction, where the attributive reading of a definite NP picks out whatever that NP is true of, whereas the referential reading picks out a specific entity intended by the speaker, although we saw that there are problems with claiming that only one of these readings is referential. Much depends on what it means to know someone's or something's identity, and that is – not surprisingly – a tricky question.

All of this led into a discussion of possible worlds and discourse models. The mental model of the discourse that speakers depend on and which they assume is more or less shared between them and their interlocutors is called a discourse model, and we build it up cooperatively in the process of constructing our discourse (though we can never know whether our two models truly match). The discourse model is one possible world – that is, one possible way in which the world could be – but there are infinitely many others. These possible worlds give us a way to start talking about meaning, by defining the meaning of a proposition in terms of the set of worlds in which it's true. This is the basis for truth-conditional semantics, in which semantic meaning is any aspect of meaning that affects the truth-conditions of a sentence. As a first foray into truth-conditional semantics, we looked at the truth-conditional effects of logical operators and how these effects can be shown in a truth table. Differences between the meanings of these operators as shown in the truth tables and their meanings as used in natural language will be explained by pragmatics.

Semantics

We have discussed two aspects of semantics: lexical and sentential. Within lexical semantics, the question at hand is what it means for a word to mean something. One way to look at word meaning is through componential semantics, in which we take the meaning of a word to be built up of smaller bits of component meanings, or semantic primitives. This, however, runs into the problem that it's extremely hard to limit the number of these primitives, and if there are as many primitives as there are complex meanings built up from them, we haven't gained much. An alternative view is provided by Prototype Theory, in which we understand word meaning by means of a prototype, with membership in the denotation of a word determined by the extent to which the candidate shares the features of the prototype. The semantic features by which we evaluate a word's meaning contribute to the relationships among word meanings, and so one of the things we know when we know the meaning of a word is how it relates to other words, including relations of synonymy, antonymy, hyponymy, homonymy, and so on. Likewise, these lexical relations help give rise to parallel relations at the sentence level, such as paraphrase, entailment, ambiguity, and so on.

Because it's problematic to investigate natural-language meaning using the same natural language you're investigating, researchers have established a metalanguage for semantics. The semantic metalanguage makes use of predicates and arguments, with the arguments being either constants or variables, and the variables either free or bound by quantifiers. We looked at a couple of these quantifiers, the existential and the universal. All of this machinery provides a one-to-one form-meaning relationship between the semantic metalanguage and the meanings that it represents, and allows us to avoid the ambiguities inherent in natural language. It also gives us a way to start building up complex meanings out of simple meanings in a compositional way, with semantic meaning being built up in parallel with syntactic structure. In both semantics and syntax, the verb turns out to be crucial, determining both what several other components of the sentence can be (the arguments of the verb) and their semantic (aka thematic) roles. Verbs, in turn, can be grouped by their participation in verb alternations, which is to say that different groups of verbs give rise to different sets of allowable syntactic structures for the sentence. Finally, we paused to re-visit the notion of propositional-attitude verbs and show that they are not a threat to a compositional view of semantics. But even within a compositional approach, there's more to meaning than what is built up by the semantics, and that's where pragmatics comes in.

Pragmatics

We clearly convey meaning beyond the strict semantic meaning of what we've said, and pragmatic theory helps to explain how this is accomplished. Grice's Cooperative Principle and its maxims of Quantity, Quality, Relation, and Manner were initially intended to explain the gap between the logical meanings of the connectives and their natural-language use, but the applications of the CP go far beyond the connectives; we fulfill, flout, and violate the maxims in order to implicate meanings beyond what we have semantically stated, and our hearers use their knowledge of the CP to infer those intended meanings. Although it's easy to think of the CP as something that applies after the semantics has provided a truth-evaluable proposition, truth-values can't be established until the referents of pronouns and other noun phrases have been established – and doing that requires reference to the context, and therefore is a pragmatic issue. This means that semantic and pragmatic meaning have to be built up jointly rather than sequentially. The matter of establishing reference in English is complicated by the fact that nobody has quite yet solved the problem of the definite article; some theories of its use are based on familiarity, and some on uniqueness, but none has yet been able to handle the full range of data and predict exactly when a native English user will make use of the definite article.

Use of the definite article is also one trigger for presupposition, another phenomenon that is still controversial and has not yet been fully explained. Presuppositions have a wide range of triggers, including definites, factive verbs, change-of-state verbs, and others that this book didn't cover, but in all cases they differ from standard entailments in crucial ways, including the effect of negation. Scholars have disagreed about the status of the presupposition, and in fact whether presupposition is a semantic or a pragmatic phenomenon. If it's semantic, then either it's a type of entailment, or we need a third truth-value for propositions that are neither true nor false. Many researchers have instead approached it as a pragmatic phenomenon, which makes sense given that it's sensitive to contextual factors, but that approach is not without its problems, since we still have to explain when presuppositions arise, when they can and can't be accommodated, and how to determine what a speaker intends to presuppose and why.

This in turn leads to a need to understand speech acts, which is to say the range of actions that a speaker performs by undertaking to speak. Performatives are sentences whose very utterance (in the right context – i.e., when the felicity conditions are met) performs the act described by their semantics; direct speech acts perform the act conventionally associated with their form; and indirect speech acts perform acts neither described by their semantics nor conventionally associated with their form. Instead, in the case of indirect speech acts, hearers make use of inference, context, semantics, and the CP to determine what they believe the speaker intended – but because the hearer's understanding of the speaker is imperfect, the speaker's illocutionary force and the perlocutionary effect the utterance has on the hearer may be two entirely different things, which is one way in which miscommunication can arise.

Finally, we looked at one more way in which speakers and hearers collaborate in the making of meaning, and that is through the use of non-canonical word orders. Unlike canonical word order, these are subject to constraints on their use, and for this reason, speakers can use them to convey additional information above and beyond the semantic meaning of the utterance, including information about the status of certain phrases as representing familiar or unfamiliar information or being focused or not.

Current issues in linguistic meaning

In the preceding chapters, I've noted a couple of points where I've adopted a particular point of view; for example, this book has leaned toward a truth-conditional and compositional semantics. There are certainly other perspectives out there that I haven't had time to go into (I'll discuss one alternative to truth-conditional semantics below), and I encourage you to look into them if you delve further into semantics. I've also noted in this book several theoretical points that are still controversial and/or (to my mind) unresolved, including definiteness and presupposition, although there are researchers who would disagree with me and argue that these have indeed been resolved by one theory or another. Again, space doesn't permit me to go as deeply into these issues as I would like, but there's a great deal of information readily available, some of which I point to in the 'Further Reading' section below. Before we get there, I want to mention just a couple of ongoing controversies in a bit of detail.

I noted in Chapter 4 the relationship between Grice's maxim of Quantity and the maxim of Relation – in particular, the fact that there's a tension between saying enough and saying only what's relevant: The more a speaker says, the more likely it is that they'll include what isn't relevant, whereas the more they work to limit their contribution to what's relevant, the less they'll say. In this sense, the first and second maxim of Quantity (roughly, "say enough" and "don't say too much," respectively) are in constant tension, with Relation really being another way of warning against saying "too much" (i.e., what isn't relevant). Similarly, the maxim of Manner is, to a large extent, a further fleshing-out of what counts as either "not enough" (e.g., what's unclear or ambiguous and therefore insufficiently specified) or "too much" (e.g., what isn't brief). In view of these commonalities, Horn (1984) boils down Grice's maxims to two opposing forces that he calls the Q-Principle ("say as much as you can, given R") and the R-Principle ("say no more than you must, given Q"), while leaving Quality as, in Grice's terms, a "supermaxim" without which communication would fail altogether. In this way, Horn makes explicit the tension between 'enough' and 'not too much' that is implicit in Grice's maxims, and what Horn calls the Division of Pragmatic Labor is responsible for negotiating between the two and generating many of the implicatures that depend on them. Levinson (2000) similarly boils down the maxims to opposing forces, but distinguishes between the amount of information in a message and the amount of formal complexity (e.g., length) of the message, arriving at three heuristics for negotiating the tensions that arise within and between the categories of length (long enough, but not too long) and information (enough, but not too much).

Meanwhile, Relevance Theory (Sperber and Wilson 1986; Wilson and Sperber 2004) boils things down even further, and maintains that only one 'maxim' is needed, which they term the Principle of Relevance. For them, the act of communicating guarantees the relevance of the utterance, and human cognition is optimized to look for maximal relevance. In this view, the speaker must say enough because they are required to be as relevant as possible, and they won't say too much because that would mean saying what's irrelevant. The relevance levels of possible inferences are compared, measured in terms of 'positive cognitive effects' (roughly, changes in world view that would result from a given inference), and the inference with the greatest number of cognitive effects is deemed the most relevant and wins out. Relevance Theory also adds the notion of **explicature** to the linguist's toolkit. Recall that we came up against a problem with a purely sequential process of doing semantics before pragmatics, in that at least some pragmatic processing is required in order to resolve reference; put more simply, we can't figure out the truth-value of a sentence like *He ate breakfast* without first determining who *he* is, and that's a pragmatic question. However, we can't do ALL of the pragmatics first, since most implicatures are crucially dependent on the semantics of the sentence. This problem can be solved if we allow just enough pragmatic processing to give us a truth-evaluable proposition, which is called the **explicature**. It requires reference to the context – hence some pragmatic processing – after which semantic analysis can proceed as usual, followed by the aspects of pragmatic processing that depend in part on the semantics. The need for explicature or something similar and how to characterize it, and the precise number of pragmatic principles speakers use and how best to characterize them, are still the subject of debate.

A related issue is precisely where to draw the line between semantics and pragmatics. Recall that one of Grice's motivating goals was to retain a truth-conditional semantics in which the connectives retain their logical meanings. In this view, there's a split between 'what is said' (semantics) and 'what is implicated' (pragmatics), with truth-conditional meaning being what is said, and therefore constituting the semantic meaning of the sentence. For researchers who retain this distinction, all inferred meaning, including what's required in order to establish the truth-conditions of the sentence (for example, reference resolution), is by definition pragmatic, and it's simply not the case that the semantics is logically prior to the pragmatics. For Relevance theorists, on the other hand, anything needed to establish the truth-conditions is part of the explicature, whether it's semantic or pragmatic; in this view, a truth-conditional view of semantics is abandoned, and instead the truth-conditional meaning is the explicature, incorporating the semantics and some of the pragmatics.

Another fly in the ointment is the question of **conventional implicature**. Although in general semantic meaning is context-independent and truth-conditional while pragmatic meaning is context-dependent and non-truth-conditional, there's a relatively small class of meanings that are context-independent (so, presumably, semantic) yet non-truth-conditional (so, presumably, pragmatic). These are called conventional implicatures. For example, the sense of contrast associated with the word *but* falls into this category:

(1)   Darlene is a basketball player, but she's tall.

Suppose Darlene is both tall and a basketball player. We'd say (1) is true – but it's still an odd thing to say, because the use of *but* wrongly suggests that there's some inconsistency or contrast between being a basketball player and being tall. This contrast is part of the conventional, context-independent meaning of *but* and can't be cancelled; anytime you use *but* you're going to generate that implicature of contrast. So you'd kind of like to say it's semantic – but it doesn't affect the truth-conditions, so you'd also like to say it's pragmatic. Which side of the fence you fall on depends on whether you're going to define semantic meaning as that which is truth-conditional or whether you're going to define it as that which is conventional (i.e., independent of context).

Thus, there are three basic views of how to distinguish semantics from pragmatics: Some would say that semantic meaning is conventional and pragmatic meaning is contextual, with that distinction mapping imperfectly onto the truth-conditional/non-truth-conditional distinction. Others would say (as I've implicitly assumed in this book) that semantic meaning is truth-conditional and pragmatic meaning is non-truth-conditional, with that distinction mapping imperfectly onto the conventional/contextual distinction. (And the imperfection in the mapping between the two is demonstrated by the case of conventional implicature, where a meaning that is conventional is nonetheless not truth-conditional.) Meanwhile, Relevance theorists would say that semantics is what is conventionally 'encoded', but for them the gap between truth-conditional and conventional meaning is broader, with conventional meaning and pragmatic meaning working in tandem to produce truth-conditional meaning, i.e., the explicature.

In short, there are still many, many issues to be worked out in the theory of meaning, the factors that contribute to it, and the relationships among them. Although many of these questions seem 'academic' in the less flattering sense of the term, they have important implications in fields ranging from advertising (where presupposing a proposition can influence the hearer to accept it as uncontroversial) to the courtroom (where it's an open question what constitutes 'the whole truth and nothing but the truth' and whether omission of relevant facts counts as perjury; see Solan and Tiersma 2005 and Tiersma and Solan 2015 for fascinating work in this area). Indeed, specialists in semantics and pragmatics are frequently employed by corporations, academic testing companies, defense and intelligence agencies, and legal firms, and in many other contexts where subtle nuances of meaning can make a big difference. I hope you've seen enough of the relevant issues in this text to pique your interest in these questions, and that in the future you'll hesitate to dismiss an issue as 'just semantics'. I hope even more that you'll be a bit slower to judge another person as wrong based on a miscommunication, given the status of all communication as an imperfect, inferential, and collaborative process. And, finally, I hope that you'll consider doing a bit more reading in semantics, pragmatics, and philosophy of language, and possibly even consider becoming a researcher in one of these fields and joining the conversation.

Further reading

There are many excellent linguistics textbooks that provide a broad introduction to the field and its subfields. It would be impossible to mention a few without omitting many other very good choices, and it's safe to say that nearly every introductory linguistics textbook will cover the basic principles of linguistics, the importance of a descriptive approach, and at the very least the core subfields of phonetics, phonology, morphology, syntax, semantics, and pragmatics. Beyond that, most introductory texts will include a selection of other linguistic topics, such as language acquisition, second language learning, neurolinguistics, sociolinguistics, psycholinguistics, writing systems, historical linguistics, and language endangerment. A few excellent choices are Fromkin et al. 2014 (a good all-around introduction for beginners); Denham and Lobeck 2010 (a highly accessible introduction, with engaging side topics); O'Grady et al. 2009 (written at a slightly higher level and with excellent coverage of formal linguistics); and OSU's *Language Files* (2016, with a different set of editors for each new edition, but always with an extensive set of brief 'files' covering the full range of linguistic subfields, and with an unparalleled collection of exercises and problems).

In its focus on meaning, this book has only been able to take on a sliver of the field of philosophy of language, but Lycan 2008 is an excellent and broad-ranging textbook covering the philosophy of language in general. Ludlow 1997 and Martinich 2008 both provide very thorough volumes of important papers in the field, and Hale et al. 2017 offers a comprehensive overview of leading thinkers in this area. Classic works on reference include Mill 1867; Frege 1892; Russell 1905; Strawson 1950; and Kripke 1980, among others. Abbott 2010 is an excellent and accessible text on reference, with clear discussions of the primary competing views. To delve deeper into issues of how communication works, and the relationship between language and thought, see Reddy 1979, which may completely change the way you think about communication, and Whorf 1956, a collection of Whorf's writings, several of which address the relationship between language and thought head-on. A more contemporary view of these questions is offered by Gumperz and Levinson 1996, while McWhorter 2014 argues against Whorf and his adherents. If you've been told the

Eskimos have hundreds of words for snow, you'll enjoy the title essay in the collection *The Great Eskimo Vocabulary Hoax* (Pullum 1991).

For semantics, a reasonable next step would be an introductory semantics textbook. There are many to choose from, but some good choices are Kearns 2011 and Saeed 2016, two accessible introductory texts; Chierchia and McConnell-Ginet 2000, a very thorough and somewhat more formal introduction; and Jacobson 2014, a thorough and accessible introduction to compositional semantics. For two excellent collections of seminal papers in the field, see Portner and Partee 2002 and Davis and Gillon 2004. Davidson and Harman 1972 has not only seminal works in semantics but also related papers in philosophy and pragmatics. Coleman and Kay 1981 is a very readable paper on prototype semantics, focusing on the meaning of the word *lie* as a case in point. Levin 1993 offers a superb compendium of verb classes and alternations.

In pragmatics, you'll definitely want to read Grice 1975. Several excellent textbooks on pragmatics are available, including Levinson 1983 (a bit dated, but it's the granddaddy of them all), Birner 2013, and Huang 2015. Davis 1991 brings together many of the seminal papers in pragmatics. There are also several excellent collections of more current papers covering the full range of topics in pragmatics, including Horn and Ward 2004, Allan and Jaszczolt 2015, and Huang 2017. For speech acts, Austin 1962 is a short but engaging classic. Regarding accommodation, Lewis 1979 is required reading. To dig deeper into theories of implicature since Grice, see Horn 1984, Sperber and Wilson 1986, and Levinson 2000. Abbott 2016 is one of several excellent papers by Abbott on definiteness and the various approaches different scholars have taken toward it. Birner and Ward 1998 presents a straightforward, empirically based theory of non-canonical word order in English, and Prince 1981 and 1992 are important papers in this area.

For more in-depth introductions to individual topics within linguistics, written at an accessible level, watch for additional titles in the Routledge Guides to Linguistics series.

References

Abbott, B. 2002. Presuppositions as nonassertions. *Journal of Pragmatics* 32:1419–37.

Abbott, B. 2008. Presuppositions and common ground. *Linguistics and Philosophy* 21:523–38.

Abbott, B. 2010. *Reference*. Oxford: Oxford University Press.

Abbott, B. 2016. The indefiniteness of definiteness. In T. Gamerschlag, D. Gerland, R. Osswald, and W. Petersen, eds., *Frames and Concept Types*. New York: Springer.

Allan, K. and K.M. Jaszczolt. 2015. *The Cambridge Handbook of Pragmatics*. Cambridge: Cambridge University Press.

Austin, J.L. 1962. *How to Do Things With Words: The William James Lectures Delivered at Harvard University in 1955*. J.O. Urmson and M. Sbisà, eds. Oxford: Clarendon Press.

Birner, B.J. 2006. Inferential relations and noncanonical word order. In B.J. Birner and G. Ward, eds., *Drawing the Boundaries of Meaning: Neo-Gricean Studies in Pragmatics and Semantics in Honor of Laurence R. Horn*. Amsterdam: John Benjamins. 31–51.

Birner, B.J. 2013. *Introduction to Pragmatics*. Oxford: Wiley-Blackwell.

Birner, B.J. and G. Ward. 1998. *Information Status and Noncanonical Word Order in English*. Amsterdam: John Benjamins.

Chierchia, G. and S. McConnell-Ginet. 2000. *Meaning and Grammar: An Introduction to Semantics*, 2nd ed. Cambridge, MA: MIT Press.

Coleman, L. and P. Kay 1981. Prototype semantics: The English word *lie*. *Language* 57.1:26–44.

Davidson, D. and G. Harman, eds. 1972. *Semantics of Natural Language*. Boston: Reidel.

Davis, S., ed. 1991. *Pragmatics: A Reader*. Oxford: Oxford University Press.

Davis, S. and B.S. Gillon, eds. 2004. *Semantics: A Reader*. Oxford: Oxford University Press.

Denham, K. and A. Lobeck. 2010. *Linguistics for Everyone: An Introduction.* Boston: Wadsworth.

Donnellan, K.S. 1966. Reference and definite descriptions. *Philosophical Review* 75:281–304.

Frege, G. 1892. Über Sinn und Bedeutung. *Zeitschrift für Philosophie und Philosophische Kritik* 100:25–50.

Fromkin, V., R. Rodman, and N. Hyams. 2014. *An Introduction to Language,* 10th ed. Boston: Wadsworth.

Grice, H.P. 1957. Meaning. *The Philosophical Review* 66.3:377–88.

Grice, H.P. 1975. Logic and conversation. In P. Cole and J. Morgan, eds., *Syntax and Semantics 3: Speech Acts.* New York: Academic Press. 41–58.

Gumperz, J.J. and S.C. Levinson. 1996. *Rethinking Linguistic Relativity.* Cambridge: Cambridge University Press.

Hale, B., C. Wright, and A. Miller, eds. 2017. *A Companion to the Philosophy of Language,* 2nd ed. Oxford: Wiley-Blackwell.

Horn, L.R. 1972. *On the Semantic Properties of Logical Operators in English.* Ph.D. dissertation, UCLA.

Horn, L.R. 1984. Toward a new taxonomy for pragmatic inference: Q-based and R-based implicature. In D. Schiffrin, ed., *Meaning, Form, and Use in Context: Linguistic Applications.* Washington, DC: Georgetown University Press. 11–42.

Horn, L.R. and G. Ward, eds. 2004. *The Handbook of Pragmatics.* Malden, MA: Blackwell.

Huang, Y. 2015. *Pragmatics.* Oxford: Oxford University Press.

Huang, Y., ed. 2017. *The Oxford Handbook of Pragmatics.* Oxford: Oxford University Press.

Jacobson, P. 2014. *Compositional Semantics: An Introduction to the Syntax/ Semantics Interface.* Oxford: Oxford University Press.

Kearns, K. 2011. *Semantics,* 2nd ed. New York: Palgrave Macmillan.

Kripke, S. 1980. *Naming and Necessity.* Cambridge, MA: Harvard University Press.

Levin, B. 1993. *English Verb Classes and Alternations: A Preliminary Investigation.* Chicago: University of Chicago Press.

Levinson, S.C. 1983. *Pragmatics.* Cambridge: Cambridge University Press.

Levinson, S.C. 2000. *Presumptive Meanings: The Theory of Generalized Conversational Implicature.* Cambridge, MA: MIT Press.

Lewis, D. 1979. Scorekeeping in a language game. *Journal of Philosophical Language* 8:339–59.

Ludlow, P., ed. 1997. *Readings in the Philosophy of Language.* Cambridge, MA: MIT Press.

Lycan, W.G. 2008. *Philosophy of Language: A Contemporary Introduction,* 2nd ed. New York: Routledge.

Martinich, A.P. 2008. *The Philosophy of Language*, 5th ed. Oxford: Oxford University Press.

McWhorter, J.H. 2014. *The Language Hoax: Why the World Looks the Same in Any Language*. New York: Oxford University Press.

Mill, J.S. 1867. *A System of Logic*. London: Longmans.

O'Grady, W., J. Archibald, M. Aronoff, and J. Reese-Miller. 2009. *Contemporary Linguistics*, 6th ed. Boston: Bedford/St. Martins.

Ohio State University Department of Linguistics. 2016. *Language Files: Materials for an Introduction to Language and Linguistics*, 12th ed. Columbus, OH: Ohio State University.

Portner, P. and B. Partee, eds. 2002. *Formal Semantics: The Essential Readings*. Oxford: Blackwell.

Prince, E.F. 1981. Toward a taxonomy of given/new information. In Peter Cole, ed., *Radical Pragmatics*. New York: Academic Press. 223–54.

Prince, E.F. 1992. The ZPG letter: Subjects, definiteness, and information-status. In S. Thompson and W. Mann, eds., *Discourse Description: Diverse Analyses of a Fundraising Text*. Amsterdam/Philadelphia: John Benjamins. 295–325.

Pullum, G. 1991. *The Great Eskimo Vocabulary Hoax and Other Irreverent Essays on the Study of Language*. Chicago: University of Chicago Press.

Putnam, H. 1975. The meaning of meaning. In *Mind, Language and Reality; Philosophical Papers Volume 2*. Cambridge: Cambridge University Press. 215–71.

Reddy, M.J. 1979. The Conduit Metaphor: A case of frame conflict in our language about language. In A. Ortony, ed., *Metaphor and Thought*. Cambridge: Cambridge University Press. 284–324.

Russell, B. 1905. On denoting. *Mind* 14.56:479–93.

Saeed, J.I. 2016. *Semantics*, 4th ed. Oxford: Wiley-Blackwell.

Sapir, E. 1929. The status of linguistics as a science. In E. Sapir, 1958, *Culture, Language and Personality*, D.G. Mandelbaum, ed. Berkeley, CA: University of California Press.

Solan, L.M. and P.M. Tiersma. 2005. *Speaking of Crime: The Language of Criminal Justice*. Chicago: University of Chicago Press.

Sperber, D. and D. Wilson. 1986. *Relevance: Communication and Cognition*. Cambridge, MA: Harvard University Press.

Stalnaker, R. 1974. Pragmatic presuppositions. In M. Munitz and P. Unger, eds., *Semantics and Philosophy*. New York: New York University Press. 197–214.

Strawson, P.F. 1950. On referring. *Mind* 59:320–44.

Strawson, P.F. 1952. *Introduction to Logical Theory*. London: Methuen.

Tiersma, P.M. and L.M. Solan. 2015. *The Oxford Handbook of Language and Law*. Oxford: Oxford University Press.

Whorf, B.L. 1940. Science and linguistics. *MIT Technology Review* 42:229–31. [reprinted in Whorf 1956.]

Whorf, B.L. 1941. The relation of habitual thought and behavior to language. In L. Spier, ed., *Language, Culture and Personality: Essays in Memory of Edward Sapir*. Menasha, WI: Sapir Memorial Publication Fund. 75–93. [reprinted in Whorf 1956.]

Whorf, B.L. 1956. *Language, Thought and Reality*. J.B. Carroll, ed. Cambridge, MA: MIT Press.

Wilson, D. and D. Sperber. 2004. Relevance Theory. In Horn and Ward 2004.

Index